Law Made Fun Through Harry Potter's Adventures

99 Lessons
in Law from the
Wizarding World
For Fans of All Ages

Karen Morris, Esq.
Bradley S. Carroll, Esq.

www.lawmadefun.com

Cover design by Carol Bassett

ISBN: 1461157234
ISBN-13: 9781461157236

First Edition: July, 2011

Printed by CreateSpace

DEDICATIONS

I dedicate this book to Jamie, my wonderful
little sister from the Big Brother/Big Sister
program, and her three young children —
Jason, Bianca and Kenny. Happily, they are
all destined to become Harry Potter fans.

Karen

This book is dedicated with love to my wife
who introduced me to the world of Harry
Potter, and to my sons Alex and Benjamin
whose lives have been touched in many
ways by the Harry Potter phenomena.

Brad

TABLE OF CONTENTS

Page

I.   INTRODUCTION 1

II.   FAMILY RELATIONSHIPS 5

    CHAPTER 1   CUSTODY OF ORPHAN
                 CHILDREN 6

    CHAPTER 2   ABANDONMENT OF
                 INFANTS.................................... 9

    CHAPTER 3   CHILD NEGLECT AND
                 ABUSE 11

    CHAPTER 4   RESTRICTIONS ON
                 MINORS..................................... 15

    CHAPTER 5   INCEST.................................... 20

III. SCHOOLS AND THE LAW................................... 21

    CHAPTER 6   COMPULSORY
                 EDUCATION 22

    CHAPTER 7   IN LOCO PARENTIS 24

    CHAPTER 8   CORPORAL
                 PUNISHMENT....................... 29

    CHAPTER 9   BULLYING.............................. 33

    CHAPTER 10   STUDENTS' PRIVACY
                 RIGHTS 36

    CHAPTER 11   AMERICANS WITH
                 DISABILITIES ACT 38

    CHAPTER 12   BANNED BOOKS 40

    CHAPTER 13   CHEATING/CODES OF
                 CONDUCT 42

TABLE OF CONTENTS
(continued)

Page

CHAPTER 14   DUE PROCESS FOR
              STUDENTS AT
              SUSPENSION HEARINGS 44

CHAPTER 15   TEACHER TENURE 48

CHAPTER 16   SCHOOL BOARD.................................. 50

IV.   CRIMES AGAINST PEOPLE 52

CHAPTER 17   MURDER 53

CHAPTER 18   ASSISTED SUICIDE 54

CHAPTER 19   ASSAULT AND BATTERY
              – THE CRIME 56

CHAPTER 20   KIDNAPPING 58

CHAPTER 21   IDENTITY THEFT 60

CHAPTER 22   HATE CRIMES...................................... 62

CHAPTER 23   ENDANGERING THE
              WELFARE OF AN
              INCOMPETENT PERSON 65

V.   CRIMES AGAINST PROPERTY.. 67

CHAPTER 24   LARCENY.. 68

CHAPTER 25   ROBBERY.. 70

CHAPTER 26   UNAUTHORIZED USE OF
              A MOTOR VEHICLE 72

CHAPTER 27   TRESPASS 74

CHAPTER 28   BURGLARY.. 77

TABLE OF CONTENTS
(continued)

Page

CHAPTER 29   CRIMINAL MISCHIEF/VANDALISM 79

CHAPTER 30   ARSON 81

CHAPTER 31   FORGERY 82

VI.   CRIMINAL BEHAVIOR - MISCELLANEOUS 84

CHAPTER 32   LOITERING 85

CHAPTER 33   DISTURBING THE PEACE/DISORDERLY CONDUCT 87

CHAPTER 34   RIOT 89

CHAPTER 35   MAIL ABUSE 90

CHAPTER 36   CRUELTY TO ANIMALS 92

CHAPTER 37   ILLEGAL POSSESSION OF CULTURAL ARTIFACTS 94

CHAPTER 38   ILLEGAL POSSESSION OF DRUGS 97

CHAPTER 39   GAMBLING 98

CHAPTER 40   FORTUNE TELLING 100

CHAPTER 41   ESCAPE 102

CHAPTER 42   HINDERING PROSECUTION 104

CHAPTER 43   AIDING AND ABETTING 106

CHAPTER 44   CONSPIRACY 109

TABLE OF CONTENTS
(continued)

Page

CHAPTER 45   MISCONDUCT OF PUBLIC OFFICIALS 111

CHAPTER 46   SELF-DEFENSE AND DEFENSE OF OTHERS 113

CHAPTER 47   INSANITY DEFENSE 115

CHAPTER 48   JUSTIFICATION 118

CHAPTER 49   EAVESDROPPING AND WIRETAPPING 120

VII.   RIGHTS WHEN CHARGED WITH A CRIME (CONSTITUTIONAL LAW, PART I)............................... 123

CHAPTER 50   INVESTIGATIONS 124

CHAPTER 51   SEARCH AND SEIZURE.................... 127

CHAPTER 52   ARREST 130

CHAPTER 53   BOUNTY HUNTERS 133

CHAPTER 54   INFORMANTS AND IMMUNITY... 136

CHAPTER 55   NOTICE AND OPPORTUNITY TO BE HEARD.. 139

CHAPTER 56   RIGHT TO AN UNBIASED JUDGE... 141

CHAPTER 57   RIGHT TO AN ATTORNEY............... 144

CHAPTER 58   EVIDENCE... 146

CHAPTER 59   INNOCENT UNTIL PROVEN GUILTY............................... 149

TABLE OF CONTENTS
(continued)

Page

CHAPTER 60   SELF-INCRIMINATION/
CONFESSIONS.................................... 151

CHAPTER 61   LIE DETECTORS 154

CHAPTER 62   APPEALS 156

CHAPTER 63   SENTENCING 157

CHAPTER 64   DEATH PENALTY 159

VIII.   NON-CRIMINAL WRONGS (TORTS) 162

CHAPTER 65   NEGLIGENCE 163

CHAPTER 66   DEFAMATION 165

CHAPTER 67   FALSE IMPRISONMENT.................... 169

CHAPTER 68   FRAUD.. 171

CHAPTER 69   INVASION OF PRIVACY 173

CHAPTER 70   ASSAULT AND BATTERY
– THE TORTS..................................... 175

CHAPTER 71   ASSUMPTION OF RISK..................... 177

CHAPTER 72   INFORMED CONSENT 180

IX.   INDIVIDUAL FREEDOMS
(CONSTITUTIONAL LAW, PART II) 182

CHAPTER 73   FREEDOM OF SPEECH 183

CHAPTER 74   FREEDOM OF THE PRESS................. 186

CHAPTER 75   FREEDOM OF ASSEMBLY 189

CHAPTER 76   EQUAL PROTECTION 192

CHAPTER 77   ABOLITION OF SLAVERY 194

TABLE OF CONTENTS
(continued)

Page

CHAPTER 78   GUN CONTROL 196

CHAPTER 79   MARTIAL LAW 198

X.   CONTRACTS.. 200

CHAPTER 80   FREEDOM OF CONTRACT................ 201

CHAPTER 81   CONSIDERATION 203

CHAPTER 82   WRITTEN AND ORAL AGREEMENTS.................................... 205

CHAPTER 83   WARRANTIES 207

XI.   MISCELLANEOUS TOPICS 209

CHAPTER 84   WILLS AND INHERITANCE.................................... 210

CHAPTER 85   BURIAL AND GRAVE ISSUES 215

CHAPTER 86   EMPLOYMENT ISSUES 217

CHAPTER 87   VETERANS' BENEFITS 220

CHAPTER 88   PERFORMANCE-ENHANCING DRUGS 222

CHAPTER 89   MARRIAGE 224

CHAPTER 90   GOVERNMENT.................................... 227

CHAPTER 91   LEGAL TENDER................................. 230

CHAPTER 92   ANIMAL USE FOR MEDICAL RESEARCH 231

CHAPTER 93   DANGEROUS AND EXOTIC ANIMALS............................. 233

TABLE OF CONTENTS
(continued)

Page

CHAPTER 94   DUE PROCESS FOR
ANIMALS 235

CHAPTER 95   DANGEROUS AND
EXOTIC PLANTS 237

CHAPTER 96   LOBBYING 240

CHAPTER 97   GOVERNMENT-
MANDATED
REGISTRATION 242

CHAPTER 98   EMERGENCY
RESTRICTIONS 244

CHAPTER 99   IMPORT/EXPORT LAWS 246

APPENDICES 249

Appendix A   INTRODUCTION TO LAW 250

Appendix B   DIFFERENCES BETWEEN
CIVIL AND CRIMINAL
LAW 252

Appendix C   CRIMINAL LAW ISSUES 254

Appendix D   COURT JURISDICTION 256

I.

INTRODUCTION

INTRODUCTION

Welcome fellow Harry Potter fans! If you love wizards, witches, and Hogwarts, and if you are curious about the law, this book is for you. It explores the intersection of Harry Potter's adventures and the law of our society. You may have read all the books in the series, repeatedly seen all the movies, and yet never realized that the story includes many, many legal issues. Or you may have identified legal matters in the books but never knew if they were true-to-life. This book will expand your horizons by introducing you to the law using Harry's world and his adventures as the guide.

The Wizarding world's creator – J.K. Rowling – appears to have a fascination with all things legal. She wove into her incredibly captivating story many vignettes that implicate the law. If you think about it, you realize the law had to be an essential component of the series because what J.K. Rowling did was to create an entire new society in an alternate universe. For a society to function orderly and for people to live together without chaos, there must be laws and rules for people to follow. Thus, law is a critical component for any civilized society, including ours and Harry's. Law is what differentiates anarchy from order and civility. Law imposes penalties – such as jail or fines – for illegal acts. Law also provides a mechanism to settle disputes among people and protect our rights as individuals.

In the Wizarding world, there is a Ministry of Magic which functions as the government. The Ministry, among other things, establishes and enforces laws through its various departments. This structure in which that government creates and enforces the law is similar to how government functions in the Muggle world. Likewise, many of the laws in Rowling's universe are similar to those in the United States of America. This makes easy the undertaking of this book – to equate laws referenced in the Harry Potter story to the laws that all of us must follow in this country. This book uses the twists and turns in the experiences of our favorite, and some not-so-favorite, characters as case examples to illustrate legal principles.

How to Use This Book

This book contains 11 modules, 10 of which cover a major category of law and consist of numerous chapters that have a common theme. The chapters within the module address a specific area of law and include the following components:

- **HP Facts.** This section contains Harry Potter story sketches relevant to the particular law addressed in the chapter. After each HP Fact, there will be a reference to the applicable Harry Potter book and chapter from which the facts were extracted.*

- **Muggle Law.** This feature provides easily understood explanations of the law of our (Muggle) society.

- **Application to HP Facts.** This part discusses the Muggle law's application to the book's characters and story line. This information eases the learning process by involving plots and characters that fascinate us all.

- **Other Areas of Law Implicated by These Facts** will identify other legal topics discussed in this book that apply to the same **HP Facts**.

---

* For easy reference, the Harry Potter books have been abbreviated as follows: *Sorcerer's Stone (SS)*; *Chamber of Secrets (COS)*; *Prisoner of Azkaban (POA)*; *Goblet of Fire (GOF)*; *Order of the Phoenix (OOP)*; *Half Blood Prince (HBP)*; and the *Deathly Hallows (DH)*. So, for example, if at the end of **HP Facts** you see (*GOF–5*), you can find the reference in *Harry Potter and the Goblet of Fire*, Chapter 5.

At the end of this book, there are four Appendices that provide more detailed information regarding some of the terms and laws discussed throughout the chapters.

One of the exciting, yet confounding, characteristics of the law is that it frequently changes. Legislators pass new statutes, and judges interpret the law with new insights. The references to law in this book relate to the law in effect as of the time of publication.

For ease of reading, we have used the pronoun "he" throughout the book in lieu of the somewhat awkward alternatives of "he or she" or "s/he." Ideally, a pronoun referring to one person would exist that is gender-neutral, but such is not the case. So please know that our use of "he" is intended, like the law, to be all inclusive without indicating favor or preference for one gender or the other.

So come extend your encounters with your Wizarding pals and add an additional dimension to your reading – lessons in law from Harry's adventures.

Enjoy!!

II.

FAMILY
RELATIONSHIPS

CHAPTER 1

CUSTODY OF ORPHAN CHILDREN

Guardian Angel Missing

HP Facts: After the death of Harry's parents, Professor Dumbledore arranged for Harry to live with his only surviving relatives – Aunt Petunia, Uncle Vernon, and Cousin Dudley, known collectively as the Dursleys. Dumbledore, Professor McGonagall, and Hagrid left infant Harry on the Dursleys' doorstep wrapped in a blanket in the middle of the night. Dumbledore tucked a note inside Harry's blanket explaining the circumstances of his arrival. The Dursleys were not pleased to have him. They assigned him to a room which was a cupboard under the stairs, notwithstanding the availability of an unused guest bedroom upstairs. Harry was ignored, ill-fed, belittled, and bullied. The Dursleys did everything possible to suppress his Wizarding traits. (*SS-1, 2*)

Additional HP Facts: Desperate and broke one New Year's Eve night, Tom Riddle's mother Merope staggered into a Muggle orphanage in London, gave birth and then died within the hour. Having no other relatives available to raise him, Riddle grew up and stayed in that orphanage until he was visited by Professor Dumbledore who informed Riddle that he was a wizard and that he had been accepted into Hogwarts. (*HBP-13*)

Muggle Law: *Guardian.* When a child's parents are killed, the law wants to be sure the child has food to eat, a safe home, and at least one adult who is concerned for him. The law arranges for someone or an orphanage to accept that responsibility. The person who does so is called a *guardian.* Sometimes several people want to be guardian; other times, no one is willing. In either circumstance, the law provides a process to determine who will take on this role.

Selection of a Guardian. Guardians are selected by a judge. Prior to making a decision, the judge considers several factors.

One is the parents' wishes as expressed in a *will* (a document that states who will get a person's property after death), if the parents created one. So, for example, the parents might identify the child's favorite aunt as the desired caregiver after the parents' death. The judge, however, is not bound by the parents' preference. The judge must determine if the person identified in the will is competent and willing to care for the child. The life of an adult is greatly altered when accepting responsibility for a youngster. Many would-be guardians welcome the undertaking and thrive in performing the duties. Others are not interested and become resentful. Unfortunately for Harry, the Dursleys were in the latter category.

If parents die without a will, or if they did not include in their will a preference for a guardian, the judge will make the selection without the benefit of parental input. Preference will be given to relatives of the child. If there are no qualified aunts, uncles, older cousins or the like, a person other than a relative can be chosen.

Investigation and Home Study. Prior to deciding who will be guardian, the judge will require an investigation be made of the people being considered. The purpose of the inquiry is to determine if they can handle the responsibilities of caring for a child. Many aspects of the candidates' lives are examined, including criminal background, medical history, education and career, finances, marital status, and a fingerprint check. This latter probe compares the prints of would-be guardians with those of known criminals. If there is a match, the person is disqualified as a guardian. Also, the investigation typically includes an inspection of the home where the child would be living to see if it is suitable. This inspection is called a *home study.*

Application to HP Facts: Dumbledore would not have been able to choose Harry's guardian in the Muggle world. Instead, a judge would have made the decision. Since the Dursleys were his only living relatives, they would have been given priority. However, the Dursleys might not have passed the home study. One look at the cupboard under the stairs as the room Harry would be assigned, and the investigator would have determined it was not a suitable place for a child. Also, the Dursleys' strong fear and dislike of "Harry's type" (wizards) suggests they could not provide the unconditional love every child needs. This lack of love would be another reason to disqualify them.

Concerning Riddle, no relatives were available to raise him and apparently no other individual came forward to be his guardian. A suitable placement for an orphan in these circumstances is a licensed orphanage.

* * * * * * * * * * * * *

Other Areas of Law Implicated by These Facts
Abandonment of Infants
Child Abuse

CHAPTER 2

ABANDONMENT OF INFANTS

No Babes in the Woods, Please

HP Facts: After the death of Harry's parents, infant Harry was left on the Dursleys' doorstep wrapped in a blanket in the middle of the night by Dumbledore, McGonagall, and Hagrid. Dumbledore attached a letter explaining the circumstances of Harry's arrival. A few hours passed before Harry was found by the Dursleys. (*SS-1*)

Muggle Law: Sadly, mothers sometimes abandon their babies. Sometimes the infant is left in a dumpster or on a stranger's doorstep. Often the child is not discovered and so is left to die. Abandonment of a child by a mother or other person legally responsible for the child is a crime in most states. "Abandonment" is defined as permanently deserting the child. The crime is usually classified as a felony and may subject the mother to several years in jail.

Most states have adopted a law that seeks to save the lives of abandoned infants. These statutes protect the mother or guardian from prosecution if she or he leaves the child with an emergency care provider, such as hospital emergency room workers, police officers, or fire fighters. These folks are qualified to address any immediate medical needs of the child.

Application to HP Facts: None of the Hogwarts' staff who accompanied Harry to the Dursleys was his mother. They had, however, accepted responsibility for his safekeeping. Because they left him on the Dursleys' front steps in the middle of the night and did not wait for the Dursleys to find him, they could be prosecuted for the crime of abandonment of an infant.

* * * * * * * * * * * * * *

Other Areas of Law Implicated by These Facts
Custody of Orphan Children

CHAPTER 3

CHILD NEGLECT AND ABUSE

Not Nice

HP Facts: At the beginning of the series, Aunt Petunia and Uncle Vernon ever-so-begrudgingly became Harry's guardians. If the Dursleys have any affection for Harry, they totally fail to show it. Instead, their actions demonstrate great dislike for him. The Dursleys ignore and ridicule him in favor of their bullying son, Dudley. Uncle Vernon repeatedly complained in Harry's presence about the cost to feed and care for him. To save money, Mr. Dursley sometimes denied Harry meals. For his birthday Harry usually received no gift. On his 10th birthday, the Dursleys relented and gave Harry a present – a coat hanger and a pair of Uncle Vernon's socks! Compare this to Dudley's birthday celebrations – the Dursleys treated him to a day's outing with a friend. Harry was left behind.

Dudley, too, repeatedly mistreated Harry. Dudley punched Harry in the nose, sometimes breaking Harry's distinct circular-rimmed glasses. Harry's aunt and uncle did not scold Dudley or repair the spectacles, except with unsightly tape, causing Harry great embarrassment. At times, the Dursleys ignored Harry altogether, acting as though he did not exist.

After Harry's wizard background was disclosed, circumstances worsened. Aunt Petunia called him a "freak" and "abnormal" and continually belittled him, yelled at him, or ignored him. On at least one occasion, Uncle Vernon grasped Harry tightly around Harry's throat. (*OOP-1*) On another occasion, Uncle Vernon installed bars on Harry's window and locked him in his room for days at a time. While there, Harry was fed only meager meals through a cat flap that Uncle Vernon fitted on the door. While confined in this way, Harry was only allowed to use the bathroom twice a day. (*COS-2*)

Muggle Law: The law recognizes the importance in every child's life of parents or guardians who provide food, a home, and love. The law also recognizes that, sadly, parents and guardians sometimes fall short of this standard. If a child is abused or neglected by a parent or guardian, the law authorizes removal of the child from the home and relocation of the youngster to a safer place.

Child neglect and child abuse have separate meanings. Both involve mistreatment of a child. Generally, abuse refers to more serious maltreatment than neglect and can result in stricter penalties.

Neglect. A child is neglected if his parent or guardian leaves him home alone without needed supervision or fails to provide adequate clothing such as a heavy coat in the winter, or fails to secure the youngster's regular attendance in school. Another form of neglect is emotional. This includes such behaviors as repeatedly belittling the child; disregarding the child's emotional needs such as love, companionship, and assistance with customary problems that children confront; or ridiculing a child's loved parent.

Abuse. A child is abused if the parent or guardian intentionally inflicts physical injury on the youngster, allows another person to inflict such injury, or engages in sexual conduct with him. Parents who beat their children or touch them inappropriately are committing child abuse. In numerous states, abuse also includes placing the child in immediate risk of injury, such as dangling a baby out of a window.

Family Court (also called *juvenile court* or *orphans court* depending on the state). Each state has an agency responsible for investigating child abuse and neglect cases. If the investigator concludes that a child is neglected or abused, the case is referred to a family court judge who has several options. The judge can require the parents to attend parenting classes, go to counseling, attend drug or alcohol treatment programs, or participate in an anger management program. While the parents are in treatment, the judge can direct that the child remain in the home with periodic monitoring by a court-appointed counselor or remove the child from the parents' home and place him in *foster care*, depending on the level of risk to the child. In foster care, the child is cared for by a willing family, preferably a relative or others who have a relationship with the child. If such placement is not available, the foster family could be someone not previously known to the child. During foster care, the parents are often granted permission by the judge to visit with the child. The judge may require such visits be supervised by a court representative. A typical goal of the judge is to eventually reunite the child with his parents, if possible to do so safely. If, however, the parents are not able to resolve their problems, the judge can end the parents' legal rights to the child. This legal action is called *termination of parental rights.*

Adoption. If parental rights are terminated, the child can be *adopted* by another family. This means a new family accepts the child as their own and becomes legally responsible to provide for his needs.

If the child is old enough to understand the circumstances, the judge is likely to consider the wishes of the child as to who should become his adopted family.

Attorney for the Child. In abuse, neglect, and adoption cases the court will appoint a lawyer for the child, called a *law guardian* in some states. The lawyer's role is to help the child understand what is occurring in and out of court and to ensure the child's interests are presented and considered by the judge.

Criminal Consequences. Abuse and neglect can also constitute a crime. A parent who abuses or neglects a child may be guilty of the crime of Endangering the Welfare of a Child, a misdemeanor in most states. If the abuse results in serious injury, the crime may be a felony.

13

Application to HP Facts: The Dursleys' treatment of Harry certainly constituted neglect. They deprived him of adequate food, sleeping space, and clothing. They regularly demeaned him and his parents. The Dursleys totally ignored his emotional needs for companionship and love.

Arguably, the Dursleys' conduct also constituted abuse. Harry might have suffered injury from the inadequate food he was given or the limited frequency of bathroom access. When Uncle Vernon put his hands around Harry's neck, Harry was in potential jeopardy of suffocating. Living in the closet under the stairs could have resulted in stunted growth or other injury.

* * * * * * * * * * * * * *

Other Areas of Law Implicated by These Facts

Abandonment of Infants
Assault and Battery – The Crime
Assault and Battery – The Torts
Bullying
Custody of Orphan Children

CHAPTER 4

RESTRICTIONS ON MINORS

Sweet Seventeen

HP Facts: In the Wizarding world, the age a youngster legally becomes an adult is 17. This is referred to throughout the books as "of age." To ensure that young wizards and witches do not perform underage magic away from school, the Ministry of Magic puts an enchantment on them called the "Trace." If an underage witch or wizard uses magic, the Ministry knows about it immediately. *(DH-4)*

Additional HP Facts: When Harry was 15, he and Dudley were attacked by dementors a few streets from the Dursleys' house. To defend himself and his cousin against the dementors, Harry used magic by conjuring a Patronus to keep the dementors at bay. Because of his age, Harry's use of magic away from Hogwarts violated the *Decree of the Reasonable Restriction of Underage Sorcery*. As punishment, Harry was threatened with expulsion from Hogwarts. *(OOP-1,2)*

Additional HP Facts: Hogwarts students are allowed in their sixth year to take lessons on how to Apparate. However, to Apparate legally outside of class, a student must have a license, which is not issued to anyone under age 17. *(HBP-18)*

Muggle Law: In Muggle law, coming of age generally occurs at age 18. The reason for the age limits in both worlds is because young people often act without realizing all the possible consequences. A bit of maturity goes a long way towards appreciating risks and avoiding injury. To protect kids from their own youthful folly, the law restricts them from certain behaviors until they reach a specified age, called the age of majority. Among the restricted activities include the following:

Smoking. In most states, 18 is the required age to buy

cigarettes. Per the note on cigarette packages, "Smoking is harmful to your health and may cause cancer."

Voting. To vote, one must be 18. The law wants voters to make informed decisions after studying the issues and the candidates. Youngsters are less likely to do the necessary study and research. Indeed, Uncle Vernon once snickered about Harry's watching the news on television saying, "I'd like to know what he's really up to. As if a normal boy cares what's on the news – Dudley hasn't got a clue what's going on, doubt he knows who the Prime Minister is!" (The Prime Minister in England is the equivalent of the President in the United States.) *(OOP-1)*

Contracts: Prior to age 18, a person is not obligated to perform on their contracts. So if you bought a car at age 16 and later decided you would rather spend the money on a jet ski, you are in luck. You can cancel the contract and return the car. If you were 18 when you purchased the car and then wanted to cancel, you would not be legally able to do so.

Military Enrollment: Another activity foreclosed until the age of 18 is joining the military (17 year olds can join with parental approval). An enlistee should be able to fully understand the risks associated with that choice – at stake are both his own life and the country's security.

Variations on the Theme. In the Wizarding world, "of age" is 17, apparently for all purposes. In the Muggle world, the required age varies, depending on the activity. While it is 18 for many circumstances, for others it is a few years younger or older.

Alcohol and Tobacco. An activity requiring an age older than 18 is drinking alcohol. Sip your soda until age 21.

Gambling. The permissible age to gamble varies from state to state and ranges between the ages of 18 and 21.

Driving. Driving a car, a pursuit long anticipated by many youngsters, is legal beginning in most states at 16. Initially, however, adult supervision is required.

Crimes. The age of criminal responsibility varies from state to state and hovers between 16-18. If a person commits a crime and is younger than the relevant state's minimum age for criminal responsibility, his case will usually be heard in family court, rather than a criminal court. In family court, the judge is more concerned with rehabilitation than punishment. Even in criminal court, there is recognition that a young person older than 16 but not yet an adult is subject to youthful indiscretions. As a result, their criminal records may be sealed, meaning a future employer will not learn about the crime.

Sexual Activity: While <u>consensual</u> sexual activity is not illegal, a person under a specified age cannot, in the eyes of the law, consent. An adult who engages in sexual relations with someone underage violates the law. This is true even if the youngster appears to be a willing partner. In 30 states, the age of consent for sexual encounters is 16. In other states, that age is 17, 18, or 19.

Employment. The minimum age to work is 14. However, until an employee reaches age 18, the number of hours he can legally work and the type of tasks he can perform, are restricted by statute. These laws protect young workers from long work schedules that could interfere with their education and health and from potentially dangerous assignments that could affect their health and safety. For example, repairing roofs and operating an electric meat cutter require a more mature worker.

Why So Jumbled? You, no doubt, are scratching your head wondering why our lawmakers chose such a hodgepodge of ages. The answer may not be totally illuminating. The problem is this: There is no uniform age when everyone matures. If there were, identifying the appropriate time to permit an activity would be a no-brainer. But we all grow at different paces physically, mentally, and emotionally. So the various minimum ages, inexact as they are, reflect the best judgment of our legislators. Their choices were not just pulled from the air without some logic. Rather, they were based in significant part on biological information about young adult development, statistics showing the ages of people involved in various kinds of accidents, and other relevant factors.

Application to HP Facts: Consequences follow for violating age limits – both legal and non-legal. For example, Harry was almost expelled from Hogwarts for conjuring the Patronus which violated the rule against the underage use of magic. In the Muggle world, penalties for age violations include fines, loss of driving license, and unenforceable contracts. Additional penalties may be imposed on an adult who permits or forces a youngster to engage in a prohibited activity such as drinking alcohol, sexual behavior, or employment. The possible sanctions include jail time.

Principles of Principals

HP Facts: To be considered as a competitor in the Triwizard Tournament, the *Ministry of Magic* and the Heads of the three Wizarding schools imposed a minimum age of 17. Driving this age limit was the dangerous activities that make up the competition. Indeed, the contest was discontinued for awhile because, as Dumbledore told it, "the death toll mounted so high." Nonetheless, after Harry's name was mysteriously placed in the Goblet of Fire, he was chosen as a contestant although he was only 14. (*GOF-12*)

Muggle Law: In addition to the age restrictions imposed by law, guidelines, and policies, additional rules exist that suggest age limitations for other pursuits. These rules are adopted by administrators, such as school principals and school boards. Unlike statutes which are adopted by elected legislators, these rules can be waived but only for good reasons. For example, some schools have policies that encourage student athletes to be a certain age before playing rough sports such as football.

Another example is movie ratings which suggest that certain films with violent or sexual content should not be viewed by younger audiences. Compliance with the ratings is voluntary and not mandatory.

Application to HP Facts: Rules that are adopted by administrators can be waived or disregarded at the option of the administrator. If waived, no penalty is imposed when the rule is violated. For example, Harry was allowed (required) to compete in the Triwizard Tournament despite being underage. This waiver of the age rule would likewise be permissible in the Muggle world since the age requirement was imposed by the headmasters and Ministry of Magic officials, rather than a statute adopted by legislators.

* * * * * * * * * * * * * *

Other Areas of Law Implicated by These Facts

Freedom of Contract
School Board
Self-Defense and Defense of Others

CHAPTER 5

INCEST

Kissin' Cousins

HP Facts: Following Harry and Dumbledore's Pensieve trip to the "House of Gaunt," Dumbledore explains that the Gaunts were an ancient Wizarding family. They were known for their instability and violence due to their practice of marrying their own cousins. (*HBP-10*)

Muggle Law: Incest is the crime of marrying or having sexual intercourse with a person who is a close relative. This includes your ancestors (parent, grandparent, great grandparent); descendants (child, grandchild, or great grandchild); siblings (brother, sister, half brother, or half sister); or uncle, aunt, nephew, or niece. Additionally, 24 states prohibit such activities between first cousins.

The reason for the prohibition against inbreeding is that children of close relatives are more likely than offspring of non-relatives to suffer from certain physical and health problems. These include reduced fertility, higher infant death rates, slower growth rates, loss of immune system function (inability to resist diseases), and higher incidence of heart disease.

Application to HP Facts: The Gaunts' practice of marrying cousins creates the possibility of genetic defects that the crime of incest was designed to prevent. In the fictional world of J.K. Rowling, the resulting problems include the instability and violence referenced in the story and demonstrated by Merope, Morphin, and their father.

III.

SCHOOLS AND THE LAW

CHAPTER 6

COMPULSORY EDUCATION

School Rule

HP Facts: Before Harry learned that he was a wizard and would be attending Hogwarts School of Witchcraft and Wizardry, he had always attended the local public school with his cousin Dudley. Instead of continuing to secondary public school, Dudley learned that he had been accepted at the private school attended by Uncle Vernon, Smeltings. *(SS-3)*

Additional HP Facts: Before Voldemort's take-over of the Ministry of Magic, education for young wizards and witches was compulsory, but parents had choices. While almost all witches and wizards from Britain are educated at Hogwarts, parents could home-school their children or send them abroad to be educated. Once Voldemort took over the Ministry, attendance at Hogwarts became mandatory, which enabled Voldemort's regime to instruct students on Voldemort's view of the world. Also, before students could attend, they were required to prove their Blood Status. Muggle-borns were excluded from magical education. *(DH-11)*

Muggle Law: Education is a big part of the process by which a young person's potential is realized and the child, over time, becomes a responsible citizen. Without an education, a person in our society is at a significant disadvantage in many avenues of life. Recognizing this, our law guarantees to youngsters the right to receive an education. The term *compulsory education* refers to education a child is required by law to receive and governments are required to provide. All children of school age are entitled to attend public school without regard to race, color, religion, national origin, disability, or gender.

Parents have options. They can send their children to public school, send them to private school (not run by the government and usually charge tuition), or home-school them under certain circumstances. While all states have compulsory education laws, they differ as to the age of the child when the required instruction begins (ranges from 5 – 8), and the age when students can drop–out (ranges from age 16 in 26 states, to ages 17 or 18 in the remaining states). The reasons for the higher drop-out age include increasing the level of students' knowledge, decreasing juvenile crime, decreasing teen pregnancy, and encouraging students to attend college.

Penalties applied to parents who fail to enroll their children or send them to school vary from state to state. They include the following: criminal prosecution, fines, jail, community service, mediation, and referral to child protective services, which is a government agency that protects children from neglect or abuse by their parents.

Application to HP Facts: If the Ministry were in the Muggle world, it would not have been able to mandate that students attend a particular school. Rather, like the Dursleys' choice of private school for Dudley, parents of young wizards and witches would be entitled to send their kids to public school, private school, or home-school them. Further, all youngsters of school age would be entitled to attend public schools. Exclusions based on Blood Status would not be allowed.

* * * * * * * * * * * * *

Other Areas of Law Implicated by These Facts
Equal Protection

23

CHAPTER 7

IN LOCO PARENTIS

Mom's Away, the Kids Will Play – Not!

HP Facts: Harry and his buddies attend Hogwarts School of Witchcraft and Wizardry, a boarding school with a seven-year course of study. The students live on campus (at the castle) for about ten months a year. Upon arrival, Harry and the other first-year students were greeted by Professor McGonagall who explained that students would be "sorted" into houses, and their house would be like their family. She further explained that students were expected to comply with school rules. Violation of the rules can lead to detention and loss of house points. (*SS-7*)

Muggle Law: Customarily, parents are responsible for protecting, as well as disciplining, their children. The law recognizes that when young folks live at a school, they are away from the watchful eye of their moms and dads. To fill the gap, the law imposes responsibility on the school for the wellbeing of the students. The term encompassing the school's legal duties is *in loco parentis,* which means "in place of a parent."

To fulfill their responsibility, schools customarily impose rules with which students are expected to comply. They are designed to help secure the safety and welfare of the school's population. By enrolling in the school, students imply agreement to abide by the rules. Examples of such rules include: students must be vaccinated against various diseases before they can attend classes; students cannot use vulgar or offensive language; for boarding schools, they cannot be out of their rooms after curfew; and they cannot leave school grounds without notifying a teacher.

In loco parentis gives schools the authority to do the following depending on the circumstances: search student lockers and other private spaces, censor student publications if the content is inconsistent with the school's basic educational mission, and conduct random urine tests of student athletes to detect illegal drugs.

Application to HP Facts: Hogwarts stands *in loco parentis* and is therefore obligated to adopt rules and take precautions to facilitate the safety of its students. When rules are broken safety is jeopardized. The school is thus justified in punishing students for violating rules.

Field Trip

HP Facts: Students in their third year or more at Hogwarts are entitled on certain weekends to visit the Village of Hogsmead located within walking distance of the school, provided their parents or guardian signed a permission slip. Unfortunately for Harry, he was never able to secure Uncle Vernon's signature and so the school refused to allow him to go. (*POA-1*)

Muggle Law: Whenever students leave school grounds, the ability of the school to protect them is lessened. Various safety mechanisms in place at the school are not in effect elsewhere. Additionally, the people with whom students come in contact while off school premises are uncontrolled. Since these circumstances create greater risk to students than if they stayed at school, a school is wise to require permission from parents. If a student is injured while away from the campus and permission had been obtained, the school's liability would be less than if permission had not been received.

Application to HP Facts: Hogwarts' refusal to permit Harry to visit Hogsmead was consistent with its responsibilities *in loco parentis*. This duty was heightened by the fact that school officials believed Sirius Black had escaped from Azkaban to find and kill Harry.

Safety Sweep

HP Facts: Harry received a package containing a new broomstick, a Firebolt. There was no note attached so Harry did not know who had sent him this fabulous gift. Hermione, concerned that the Firebolt was sent by Sirius Black who was thought to have escaped from Azkaban Prison to find and murder Harry, told Professor McGonagall about the gift. She took the Firebolt from Harry explaining that the broom had to be checked for jinxes before he could use it. *(POA–11)*

Muggle Law: *In loco parentis* requires that schools investigate circumstances that present potential danger to students. This mandate includes the confiscation of items that may be harmful.

Application to HP Facts: McGonagall exercised the proper oversight as a representative of the school by having the Firebolt thoroughly inspected before allowing Harry to use it. This protected not only Harry but others at Hogwarts as well.

Homeward Bound?

HP Facts: In several circumstances throughout the books, Hogwarts considered closing the school and sending students home because of grave dangers lurking at the castle that the professors could not control. In the first circumstance, the heir of Slytherin was attacking Muggle-borns at Hogwarts after the Chamber of Secrets was opened. *(COS-14)* The second time occurred immediately following Professor Dumbledore's death. *(HBP-9,29)*

Muggle Law: Sometimes circumstances occur at a school that jeopardize the safety of students and cause the school to question its ability to keep pupils safe. If the threat is sufficiently serious, the responsibility of the school acting *in loco parentis* may require that it send the youngsters home.

The decision of how to proceed generally rests with the principal.

Application to HP Facts: In each instance, Hogwarts' administration recognized that Voldemort was nearby and the school's ability to ensure the safety of the students was significantly compromised. In such circumstances, the school leaders – the headmaster, assistant headmaster, and board of governors – rightly considered the best course of action to protect students' wellbeing.

Punishment Must Fit the Crime

HP Facts: Professor Umbridge was blinded to the fact that Voldemort had returned. When Harry insisted that Voldemort was back, Umbridge gave him detention. Harry was required to inscribe repeatedly on the back of his hand the phrase, "I will not tell lies." The pen she required he use broke the skin and caused both bleeding and great pain. (*OOP-13*)

Muggle Law: A school, acting *in loco parentis*, can punish noncompliance with its rules provided the disciplinary action is reasonable in light of such factors as the nature of the infraction, the penalty's potential for harm or injury, and the age of the student.

Application to HP Facts: The type of physical punishment imposed by Umbridge was not reasonable. Etching words into one's hand using a utensil that causes significant pain and a lasting scar is arguably never justified. Umbridge clearly exceeded her bounds of *in loco parentis*.

* * * * * * * * * * * * * *

Other Areas of Law Implicated by These Facts
Child Abuse
Corporal Punishment
Freedom of Speech
Negligence
School Board

CHAPTER 8

CORPORAL PUNISHMENT

Filtch, the Flogger Wannabe

HP Facts: Harry, Hermione, Draco, and Neville were found out of bed one night, thereby breaking a school rule. Professor McGonagall gave them all detention. As Filtch was escorting them to their detention with Hagrid, he commented what a pity it is that the old punishments had "died out." One such punishment was hanging students by their wrists. Filtch told Harry and the others that he keeps chains oiled in his office in case the old discipline methods are reinstated. (*SS–15*)

Additional HP Facts: While reminiscing about the days she and her husband were students at Hogwarts, Mrs. Weasley told Harry and her son Bill of a time she and Arthur were caught away from the dormitory at four in the morning. She said that Mr. Weasley "still had the marks" after being caught by the caretaker of the time, Apollyon Pringle. (*GOF –31*)

Additional HP Facts: In relaying a message to Harry that Professor Umbridge wanted to see him, Filtch told Harry that when Educational Decree Twenty-Nine is signed, Filtch will be given the authority to whip students "raw" and string them up by their ankles. (*OOP-28*) Later Filtch checked in Umbridge's office to see if the Decree was signed. He apparently found that the Decree had been and excitedly kissed the parchment on which it was written. (*OOP-29*)

Muggle Law: Corporal punishment is the deliberate infliction of pain intended to change a person's behavior or to punish him. Many countries outlaw it. In the United States, 22 states allow corporal punishment in public schools while 28 do not. Even in states where it is allowed, some school districts have rules barring this form of punishment.

Amount of Permissible Force. While excessive corporal punishment in public schools can violate a student's constitutional due process rights, the permissible use of force is substantial. Indeed, the Constitution is violated only if the force applied "caused injury so severe and disproportionate to the need for it and was so inspired by malice or sadism rather than a merely careless or unwise excess of zeal that it amounted to a brutal and inhuman abuse of official power literally shocking to the conscience."[1]

Pros and Cons. Debate rages about the appropriateness of corporal punishment.

Arguments in favor include:

- Other punishments are too gentle.
- Suspension, an oft-used alternate, is viewed by students as a vacation.
- It achieves order in the classroom and a safer school.
- Students today are more disruptive, rebellious and ill-mannered than in times past so a stricter form of punishment is indicated.
- Schools need punishment that is sure to inflict discomfort to achieve the desired end – behavior modification.

Arguments against corporal punishment include:

- It teaches children to resort to violence when angry.
- It causes injuries.
- It is used disproportionately on poor children, minorities, and those with disabilities.
- Schools that use it often have inferior academic achievement and more vandalism, truancy, violence and drop-outs.

---

[1] *Hall v. Tawney*, 621 F.2d 607 (4th Cir., 1980).

- Many alternatives have proven to be successful. These include emphasizing positive behaviors, realistic rules consistently enforced, planning with parents acceptable behavior, detentions, and in-school suspensions.
- It generates reduced self-esteem in the punished child.
- It can cause greater defiance by the child as he asserts his freedom and dignity in refusing to be controlled by corporal punishment.

Application to HP Facts: If the rules of the locality in which Hogwarts is located allows corporal punishment, Hogwarts can opt to administer it. However, the method chosen and the amount of force exerted must be reasonable. Granted, the referenced standard allows school officials to administer considerable force and pain without recourse. Nonetheless, the force or method can be excessive and cross the line into illegality. Clearly, hanging a student by his ankles would be unacceptable, as would chaining a student and inflicting injuries that are permanent and debilitating.

Crucio Excrucio

HP Facts: After Voldemort's return to power, Amycus Carrow became the Dark Arts teacher. He required students to practice the Cruciatus Curse on classmates who were in detention. *(DH – 29)*

Muggle Law: See Muggle Law above. Those rules apply here.

Application to HP Facts: The Cruciatus Curse, also know as the "torture curse," is one of the unforgivable curses. The reason is the excruciating pain it inflicts on its victims. Carrow's required use of the Cruciatus Curse on students far exceeds the permissible limits of corporal punishment.

Umbridge Wins the Round Handily

HP Facts: Following an outburst by Harry in Professor Umbridge's class concerning the return of Voldemort, Umbridge punished Harry by giving him a week of detention. When Harry arrived for his first session, Umbridge told him he would be doing lines (writing a phrase repeatedly). Umbridge then gave Harry a special quill that had no ink. When Harry began to write on the parchment, "I shall not tell lies," the words were etched into the skin on the back of his hand and also appeared on the parchment apparently in his own blood which substituted for ink. (*OOP-13*)

Muggle Law: Corporal punishment can be directed at various parts of the body. The buttocks are a common target, presumably because, although the effect is painful, this body part is less likely than some others to experience long-term physical harm.

Application to HP Facts: The back of the hand has little padding and so the required etching was particularly painful. The punishment was repeated again and again, drew blood, caused ongoing pain, and resulted in permanent markings. Pain and injury to this extent significantly exceed permissible forms of legal discipline.

* * * * * * * * * * * * * *

Other Areas of Law Implicated by These Facts
Assault and Battery – The Crime
Assault and Battery – The Torts
Freedom of Speech
In Loco Parentis

CHAPTER 9

BULLYING

Sticks and Stones Notwithstanding, Names Will Often Hurt Me

HP Facts: Throughout the series, Harry and his friends are the targets of jokes, taunts, and assaults by Harry's nemeses Draco Malfoy and his buds, Crabbe and Goyle. Examples include: mocking Harry for having "no proper family," saying that Hagrid's hut must seem like a palace to Ron "compared to what your family's used to," and commenting to Neville, "Longbottom, if brains were gold you'd be poorer than Ron Weasley, and that's saying something." Additionally, Harry was often taunted by Dudley, and his gang intimidated Harry and other youngsters in the neighborhood.

Muggle Law: Sadly, bullying is commonplace in many schools. With the popularity of social networking, bullying has also infiltrated the Internet. This phenomenon is often called *cyber bullying.* It can be particularly damaging because a bullying message can be quickly spread, not only around a school but throughout the world. Bullying includes the following nasty behaviors:

- Verbal put-downs or insults
- Intimidating gestures
- Spreading degrading rumors and gossip
- Mocking the target's private life, family, appearance, friends, and beliefs
- Provoking arguments
- Name calling
- Yelling, threatening, frightening, constantly interrupting
- Deliberately intimidating

33

- Belittling the target's ethnicity, gender, sexual preference, or a disability
- Encouraging others to turn against the person targeted

The most frequent reason students are bullied is their appearance. Other targets include weight, hair color, family, school work, lack of popularity, diligent study habits, disabilities, religion, skin color, culture, and sexual orientation.

Many schools have rules and codes of conduct that prohibit bullying. Almost all states have passed laws that prohibit bullying and impose penalties on violators. Typical provisions include the following:

- Prohibition of bullying on school grounds and during any activity conducted by the school, such as field trips
- Notification to students and parents of the prohibitions
- Requirement of training for faculty and staff on how to prevent and respond to bullying
- Creation of a new crime of bullying with strict penalties
- Mandatory reporting of incidents to school authorities and the State Education Department
- Development of a reporting method
- Inclusion of bullying awareness and sensitivity in lessons on civility, citizenship, and character education
- Increased authority for school superintendents, principals and teachers to suspend bullies
- Allocation of state money to schools to pay for the cost of implementing bullying laws

The purpose of these laws is to secure for all students a safe and welcoming environment in school, free from harassment and discrimination. These laws enable students to concentrate on their school work. Students cannot focus on learning if they are afraid of being taunted in school. Many skip school to avoid threats. Others engage in high risk behaviors such as drug use or alcohol abuse. Indeed, bullying is the leading cause of teen-age suicide.

Application to HP Facts: If Hogwarts had a rule forbidding bullying, Malfoy, Crabbe, and Goyle would face significant penalties for their demeaning conduct. Likewise, Dudley and the members of his gang could face sanctions depending on the laws of the state and city in which they act.

* * * * * * * * * * * * *

Other Areas of Law Implicated by These Facts
In Loco Parentis
School Board

CHAPTER 10

STUDENTS' PRIVACY RIGHTS

Hogsmead or Bust

HP Facts: Unfortunately for Harry, Uncle Vernon refused to sign Harry's permission slip for school trips to Hogsmead Village. Wanting to participate, Harry surreptitiously joined the student outing using his invisibility cloak to escape detection. Unluckily, Draco Malfoy caught a glimpse of Harry's head sticking out from under the cloak. Realizing he had been seen, Harry rushed back to Hogwarts hoping to arrive before Draco could report him. Alas, Draco beat Harry and reported the sighting to Professor Snape. Very unfortunately, Harry ran into Snape upon returning to the castle. Not surprisingly, Snape confronted him about being out of the castle without permission. Snape then ordered Harry to "turn out your pockets." (*POA – 14*)

Muggle Law: The United States Constitution provides a right against unreasonable searches and seizures. This means the police cannot snoop around your private property or arrest you on a whim. Rather, to search or arrest, officers need probable cause, which is a legal standard requiring a significant amount of evidence pointing toward guilt.

Students enjoy less privacy rights than others. The reason for this is that schools have a duty to maintain order and discipline and to protect the health, safety and welfare of students. To carry out these functions, school personnel have rights to search that are broader than rights of the police. Teachers or other school staff can search a student's pockets, locker, book bag, car or computer if a trustworthy basis exists to suspect that the search will turn up evidence that the student has violated either the law or school rules. For example, if one student makes a credible report to a teacher that she observed another student take an iPod from a locker, school officials can search the accused student's pockets, book bag, locker or pocketbook for evidence of the theft.

Consider now a different scenario. A girl discovers that her iPod is missing from her locker. She reports it missing but she does not have a lead on who took it. School officials might like to search all the students' lockers located nearby, hoping to uncover the missing device. However, the administrators cannot search without some basis to believe the student whose locker they want to search is in possession of the missing iPod. A random search, called informally a "fishing expedition," is not permitted. Since the school lacks a credible basis for accusing a specific person, school officials' hands are tied; they cannot search. In this circumstance, students' rights against unreasonable search and seizure keep the school at bay.

Application to HP Facts: Draco told Snape that Harry was in Hogsmead, which violated the school rule forbidding trips without written permission from a parent or guardian. Snape credited Draco's information as accurate. Snape was therefore justified in searching Harry's pockets.

* * * * * * * * * * * * * *

Other Areas of Law Implicated by These Facts
In Loco Parentis
Search and Seizure

CHAPTER 11

AMERICANS WITH DISABILITIES ACT

Bad Moon Rising

HP Facts: For Remus Lupin, the full moon is a very bad time of the month. Having been attacked and bitten as a child by werewolf Fenrir Greyback, Lupin turns into a werewolf on the night the moon shines the brightest. In the Wizarding world, werewolves are feared and shunned.

When Lupin attended Hogwarts, Professor Dumbledore learned of Lupin's circumstances. Dumbledore took steps to deal with Lupin's condition, allowing him to continue his education at Hogwarts and ultimately graduate. Dumbledore made available to Lupin the Shrieking Shack as a place to transform each month without becoming a danger to himself or anyone else. Additionally, Dumbledore arranged for the Whomping Willow to be planted at the entrance to the underground tunnel that leads to the Shack. The tree strikes mercilessly anyone who dares to try to pass it, unless the person knows the trick to immobilize it. (*POA–18*)

Muggle Law: Congress recognized in the early 1990s that people with disabilities have an uphill battle when trying to participate in various activities that are easy and commonplace for people who are able-bodied. The most common obstacle was an inability to access buildings because of stairs, narrow hallways, no grab bars in public bathrooms, elevator controls located too high to reach in a wheelchair, and more. Congress passed the Americans with Disabilities Act (ADA) in 1992 to address these issues.

The ADA prohibits discrimination against people with disabilities. It defines a "person with a disability" as someone who has a physical or mental impairment that substantially limits the ability to walk, see, hear, think or process information. Included in the statute were ways to increase access to facilities such as schools, hotels, restaurants, theatres, stadiums, and bars, as well as jobs, educational opportunities, transportation (subways, cabs, trains, planes, etc.) and housing.

As applied to education, the ADA requires that schools provide disabled students opportunities equal to their able-bodied counterparts to access schools, classrooms, and teachers. To do this, schools are required to modify their procedures and buildings wherever necessary to accommodate the needs of disabled pupils. The modifications might include adjusting rules to allow a student with difficulty processing information extra time to take a test; removing architectural barriers such as building a ramp over steps since stairs are not accessible by wheelchair; providing aids such as a sign language interpreter to translate lectures for deaf students; or offering assistive technology such as a computer that reads textbooks aloud for blind students. If, however, providing an accommodation would impose an "undue burden" on the school (for example, an excessive cost), the school can legally refuse.

Application to HP Facts: Lupin had a disability that manifested itself at least one night a month. Hogwarts would have a duty to accommodate the disability unless doing so would create an undue hardship. While the arrangements Dumbledore made for Lupin required some effort on the headmaster's part, they were not unduly burdensome.

By reserving the Shrieking Shack for Lupin's monthly transformation, Dumbledore accommodated Lupin's disability and protected Hogwarts' students from encountering a dangerous werewolf in their midst.

* * * * * * * * * * * * *

Other Areas of Law Implicated by These Facts
Equal Protection

CHAPTER 12

BANNED BOOKS

Read No Evil

HP Facts: Hermione scoured the Hogwarts library without success for information about Horcruxes. She commented, "I've been right through the restricted section and even in the most *horrible* books, where they tell you how to brew the most *gruesome* potions – nothing!" (*HBP-18*) Turns out, Professor Dumbledore had removed the books regarding Horcruxes and kept them in his office. (*DH-6*)

Additional HP Facts: Tom Riddle, wanting to live forever, sought immortality. He asked Professor Slughorn about Horcruxes. Slughorn was surprised that Riddle knew something about them and asked Riddle where he heard of them. Riddle said he encountered the term while reading. This did not ring true to Slughorn, who responded, "You'd be hard-pushed to find a book at Hogwarts that would give you details on Horcruxes, Tom." (*HBP-23*)

Additional HP Facts: Ironically, the Harry Potter books have been banned in various libraries and schools across the country. Reasons for this include the series' focus on witchcraft, wizardry, and magic. For some people, these topics are taboo.

Muggle Law: Schools and school libraries have the right to ban books that either the principal or the School Board reasonably believes jeopardizes the values and ideals the school seeks to teach. When a book is banned, it cannot be displayed, borrowed, or sold. Many schools across the country have exercised this right. Among the reasons for censoring a book is that it references death or various crimes. Many schools are concerned that these topics might influence young readers to attempt suicide or copycat crimes. Another basis for banning a book is that it contains adult language or indecent or obscene materials including sex and violence, or that the contents might scare students or expose them to potentially dangerous information for which they are not adequately prepared.

Application to HP Facts: Hogwarts was entitled to exclude books from the library that cover material the faculty and School Board find inappropriate. The topic of Horcruxes is one of advanced Dark Magic. To create a Horcrux requires murder. The prohibition was thus a reasonable exercise of discretion.

* * * * * * * * * * * * * *

Other Areas of Law Implicated by These Facts
In Loco Parentis
Murder
School Board

CHAPTER 13

CHEATING/CODES OF CONDUCT

Slughorn Gives Harry the Royal Treatment

HP Facts: Harry had not expected to be a taking Potions class in his sixth year. Professor Snape, the expected Potions professor, required an Outstanding in the fifth year Potions O.W.L. and Harry had received one grade lower – Exceeds Expectations. Turns out Professor Snape became Professor of Defense Against the Dark Arts (to Snape's great satisfaction) and Professor Slughorn taught Potions. Slughorn required only an "Exceeds Expectations" and so Harry was in. Because Harry had not planned to take the class, he had not bought the textbook. Slughorn allowed Harry to borrow one of the school's books until he could order his own. (*HBP-9*) Harry discovered that a previous owner, who called himself the Half Blood Prince, had written notes in the margins on how to improve the potions recipes. Much to Hermione's frustration, throughout the school year, Harry used the notes to get good grades.

Muggle Law: Cheating is defined as misleading, deceiving, defrauding or swindling. Cheating in school includes:

- Sharing information between students who are all taking the same test by sneaking glances at each other's paper, passing notes, text messaging, or otherwise.
- Using "cheat sheets" during a test that are hidden from the teacher on personal belongings, downloaded into a cell phone, or otherwise.
- Obtaining the questions or answer sheet before the test is given.

- Plagiarism (passing off someone else's work as your own) including downloading papers from the Internet and submitting them as the student's own.

Most schools and colleges have rules that prohibit cheating. Sometimes the rules are embodied in an honor code, which is a set of rules students are expected to live by. Typically, codes of honor demand, among other behaviors, that students act honestly in all their activities including test-taking and preparation of assignments.

Penalties for cheating in school include a warning, a grade of zero on the test or paper, a grade of zero for the course, suspension from school, or even expulsion.

Application to HP Facts: The reason Harry excelled in Potions class was not because he studied a lot, worked hard, or had natural talent in the subject. Rather, Harry's success was due to his benefitting from the work of an earlier student. This gave Harry an unfair advantage (which rightly angered Hermione), and constitutes cheating.

* * * * * * * * * * * * *

Other Areas of Law Implicated by These Facts
Due Process for Students at Suspension Hearings

CHAPTER 14

DUE PROCESS FOR STUDENTS AT SUSPENSION HEARINGS

What, When, Where, Why

HP Facts: Dementors attacked Harry in the alleyway near Privet Drive. To ward them off, Harry conjured a Patronus. This act prompted an owl to arrive with a letter requiring Harry to appear at a suspension hearing at the Ministry of Magic. He was advised that he was charged with violating the Decree of the Reasonable Restriction of Underage Sorcery and the International Confederation of Wizards Statute of Secrecy. The time and location of the hearing was included in the notice. (*OOP-2*)

Muggle Law: The law recognizes that an education is important to achieve success in life. If a school seeks to suspend or expel a student, his future is in jeopardy. Because so much is at stake, the law requires that the student be given a hearing to determine if in fact he engaged in conduct meriting such a severe penalty. The student has the right to attend the hearing and therefore the right to notice of the date, time, and location. The law mandating notice and an opportunity to be heard is called "due process" and originates in the Constitution of the United States. Due process ensures the fairness of proceedings at which a right, such as access to education, may be terminated.

Application to HP Facts: The Ministry gave Harry sufficient notice of the hearing. It included the date, time, and location. It was delivered well in advance of the hearing, giving Harry sufficient time to make arrangements to attend and prepare his defense. The letter also informed Harry of the particular laws he was accused of violating. This information enabled Harry to think about and prepare his response and gave

44

Dumbledore time to arrange for Mrs. Figg to testify. The notice, thus, satisfied due process requirements.

However, at the last minute, the Wizengamot (the group of judges deciding Harry's case) changed the location and advanced the time from 9:00 a.m. to 8:00 a.m. Notice of the altered arrangements was sent to Harry via owl only hours before the hearing and too late for Harry to receive it. This change in time without adequate notice violated Harry's due process rights. Fortunately, both he and Dumbledore found their way to the hearing timely. Had Harry not learned of the earlier schedule and had he been expelled, he could have appealed the decision based on the due process violations.

Right to Be Heard

HP Facts: During the hearing and before Dumbledore arrived, the Minister of Magic, Cornelius Fudge, asked Harry numerous questions but did not let Harry complete his answers. The dialogue went like this:

And yet you conjured a Patronus on the night of the second of August?
Yes, but --
Knowing you are not permitted to use magic outside school while you are under the age of 17?
Yes, but – -
Knowing that you were in an area full of Muggles?
Yes, but –

Only with the intervention of Dumbledore was Harry allowed to tell his side of the story without interruption and present Mrs. Figg as a witness. (*OOP-8*)

Muggle Law: During a hearing the accused has a due process right to be heard. This means he can respond to the charges and explain his actions, and cross-examine (attempt to discredit) witnesses who testify against him. The accused can also present witnesses and other evidence to convince the judges of the truth of his side of the story.

Application to HP Facts: With Dumbledore as his advocate, Harry was finally allowed the opportunity to be heard. Had the Wizengamot not permitted Harry sufficient opportunity to present his defense, the hearing would have violated Harry's due process right to be heard. In that circumstance, had the decision been to expel Harry, he could have appealed based on the due process violations.

Right to a Lawyer?

HP Facts: Dumbledore attended the hearing and spoke up on Harry's behalf. Additionally, Dumbledore arranged for Mrs. Figg to appear as a witness. She testified that, while on her way to buy cat food, she observed the dementors in the alleyway. Mrs. Figg's testimony was crucial evidence because it provided justification for Harry having used magic despite his age and despite being in view of Muggles. (*OOP-8*)

Muggle Law: Generally, due process does not require that a student at a suspension hearing be allowed active representation by an attorney or other advocate. Some schools nonetheless permit a student to have an advocate in the hearing room to assist the student in some or all aspects of the hearing.

Application to HP Facts: By allowing Dumbledore to speak for Harry during the hearing, the Wizengamot provided more due process than was required. Dumbledore's involvement illustrates the importance of an active advocate. It was the Headmaster who arranged for Mrs. Figg to testify and who reminded the judges of Clause Seven of the Decree for the Reasonable Restriction of Underage Sorcery. That is the Wizarding world's law that authorizes the use of underage magic, even in the presence of Muggles, under life-threatening circumstances.

Just Jurists

HP Facts: At Harry's hearing, actions of several judges suggested that many wanted Harry to be expelled. For example, the abruptness with which the time and location were changed, demeaning comments made by Fudge about Mrs. Figg as a witness, repeated refusal to let Harry explain the circumstances of his use of magic, and Fudge's impatience with Harry's witness ("I want this over with today, Dumbledore"), all suggest that Harry had an uphill battle in remaining as a student at Hogwarts. (*OOP-8*)

Muggle Law: Due process requires that judges at a hearing be impartial and unbiased, without any preference for one side or the other. It is unfair and a violation of due process for a judge to favor one party over the other before all the evidence has been presented.

Application to HP Facts: It appears that some of the judges in the Wizengamot were not objective and favored expulsion of Harry before the proceeding had even begun. Had the Wizengamot decided that Harry should have been ousted, an appeals judge would no doubt order a new hearing with neutral judges.

* * * * * * * * * * * * * *

Other Areas of Law Implicated by These Facts
Evidence
Innocent Until Proven Guilty
Notice and Opportunity to be Heard
Restrictions on Minors
Right to an Attorney
Right to an Unbiased Judge
Self Defense and Defense of Others

CHAPTER 15

TEACHER TENURE

Without Tenure, Position Tenuous

HP Facts: Educational Decree Twenty-Three decreed that Professor Umbridge, as the High Inquisitor of Hogwarts, had the authority to "inspect" and evaluate her fellow teachers to ensure they were complying with Ministry standards. Following her inspections of Professors Hagrid and Trelawney, she placed both of them on probation. Later, she fired Trelawney and appeared to have attempted to do the same to Hagrid. (*OOP–15,26,21*)

Muggle Law: Most employment relationships are "at-will," meaning that either the employer or the employee can terminate the relationship at any time for any reason, or for no reason, without liability. For example, if you are employed as a server at Pizza Hut and your employer decides that the restaurant is overstaffed, or you are not working up to par, or he would rather hire his nephew, he can terminate you and you would have no recourse. The employer does not have to justify the termination, prove wrongdoing on your part, or give you an opportunity to defend your position. Instead, he can fire you summarily. Likewise, if you decide you do not like the work, or you are offered a better position elsewhere, or you want a break from working, you can quit and owe nothing. Employment-at-will can have harsh results including a worker's being unexpectedly unemployed without an income.

An exception to at-will employment is tenure, a type of job security. Tenure is primarily applicable to teachers and professors and applies at some schools and not others. Once granted, tenure precludes the institution from terminating the instructor except for serious misconduct. To qualify for tenure, a professor must first serve a period of probation, approximately five years. During that time, instructors are expected to prove themselves talented teachers and meet certain benchmarks in performance. In some colleges and universities, candidates must establish themselves as a qualified researcher, publish articles in scholarly journals in their field, and obtain grant money to support the research.

Once granted, tenure can be revoked only for cause, which includes such serious infractions as professional incompetence, neglect of duty, insubordination, conviction of a felony or other offense involving moral turpitude, sexual harassment, or the like. Prior to termination, tenured faculty members are entitled to due process. This means they have the right to notice of the accusations allegedly justifying termination, a right to a hearing at which the institution must present evidence to prove the alleged wrongdoing, and an opportunity for accused faculty members to cross-examine the school's witnesses and present a defense.

Application to HP Facts: Umbridge was able to summarily terminate Trelawney and Hagrid without a hearing or other due process requirements. From this, we learn that Hogwarts' professors do not have tenure. Rather, they were employed at will. The school was therefore within its rights to terminate any professor for any reason or no reason and without notice or hearing.

We saw from Trelawney's reaction to her firing how devastating termination can be.

* * * * * * * * * * * * * *

Other Areas of Law Implicated by These Facts
Employment Issues
Notice and Opportunity to be Heard

CHAPTER 16

SCHOOL BOARD

Leaders of the Pack

HP Facts: Hogwarts School of Witchcraft and Wizardry has a board of governors comprised of 12 members. It has the power to appoint or suspend the school's headmaster. Lucias Malfoy, who is one of the governors, coerced the others on the board to sign an Order of Suspension to remove Professor Dumbledore as Headmaster. Lucias threatened to curse their families if they voted against suspension. (*COS-14,18*)

Additional HP Facts: Following Dumbledore's death, Professor McGonagall consulted other faculty on whether Hogwarts should remain open or close. Professor Flitwick, one of those advising McGonagall, reminded her that established procedures required consultation with the board of governors. (*HBP-29*)

Muggle Law: All schools have a governing body called one of several terms – school board, board of trustees, board of governors, or board of directors. The board makes policy (long range) decisions about the operation of the school. The number of members of the board varies from school to school and is typically five, seven, or nine. The board customarily meets once a month.

Among the board's specific assignments are hiring the principal, sometimes called a headmaster at a private school. The principal is responsible for running the school on a day-to-day basis and reports to the board. Other obligations of the board include reviewing the curricula (the courses offered) and teaching methods and ensuring that teachers are evaluated. In fulfilling these tasks, board members have a legal duty to act honestly and with reasonable care and diligence. This means they must study issues that arise so they are knowledgeable

50

about those issues when they express opinions and cast votes at board meetings. Additionally, board members must use their best judgment when making decisions and must be guided by what is best for the school, not for the board member, his or her children or family, or any other personal concern. All of these responsibilities together are called in law a "fiduciary" duty. Board members owe a fiduciary duty to the school.

Application to HP Facts: Concerning Dumbledore's suspension, the board of governors has the right and duty to terminate a headmaster if he is not performing to the standard set by the board. However, the decision must be made based on what is best for the school and not for board members' relatives. The Hogwarts board may have voted out of fear for the personal wellbeing of their families and not the merits of Dumbledore's service as Headmaster. Therefore, the vote should be declared null and void, and Dumbledore should remain in his position.

Concerning the decision of whether to close Hogwarts after Dumbledore's death, this is clearly the type of issue that is decided by the board of governors. The members will likely want to hear the recommendation of the headmaster (since Dumbledore is, alas, dead, the deputy headmaster), and will give it serious consideration. The ultimate decision, however, is to be made by the board.

* * * * * * * * * * * * * *

Other Areas of Law Implicated by These Facts
Assisted Suicide
In Loco Parentis
Misconduct of a Public Official
Murder

IV.

CRIMES AGAINST PEOPLE

CHAPTER 17

MURDER

Avada Kedavra

HP Facts: Throughout the Harry Potter series, numerous instances of intentional killings occur. These include: Voldemort killed Harry's parents, James and Lilly Potter (*Pre-SS*); Wormtail killed Cedric Diggory during the Triwizard Tournament (*GOF-32*); Bellatrix killed Sirius Black and Dobby (*OOP-35, DH-23*); Snape killed Dumbledore (*HBP-27*); and Voldemort killed Charity Burbage and Snape. (*DH-1,32*)

Muggle Law: The crime of murder consists of intentionally causing another person's death. It is the most serious crime that exists and, therefore, merits the most serious penalties. The sentence for murder can include life in jail and, in some states, the death penalty.

Application to HP Facts: All of the killers acted intentionally to end the life of their victims. Therefore, all the killers would be guilty of murder.

* * * * * * * * * * * * * *

Other Areas of Law Implicated by These Facts
Assisted Suicide
Death Penalty
Kidnapping

CHAPTER 18

ASSISTED SUICIDE

A Lethal Ring, Two Friends, Lights Out

HP Facts: In his quest to find and destroy Voldemort's Horcruxes, Dumbledore came upon Marvolo Gaunt's ring. This was a very valuable find because the ring was one of the Horcruxes. Dumbledore put it on his finger. The ring contained a curse of extraordinary power. To remove the curse, Dumbledore cracked the ring with the sword of Gryffindor, which destroyed the Horcrux within the ring. The curse remained in Dumbledore's hand causing it to blacken, burn, and wither. Professor Snape warned Dumbledore that the curse would strengthen and spread throughout Dumbledore's body, killing him within a year. In response, Dumbledore asked Snape to kill him at the proper time, stating that a quick, painless death was preferable "to the protracted and messy affair that it will be." Snape agreed and, as we know, he later carried out the deed. (*DH-33*)

Muggle Law: Assisted suicide encompasses action that aids in ending the life of a person who is typically terminally ill and wants to die. Most states prohibit assisted suicide and deem it a felony, punishable by a significant prison sentence. Depending on the state, the crime may be called assisting suicide, assisting self-murder, promoting suicide, or other similar title. A few states have legalized assisted suicide in very limited circumstances such as the following Oregon law. Only a doctor can assist. The patient must be terminally ill with no more than a six-month life expectancy. The patient must repeatedly request the doctor's help to end his life. The permissible assistance is to prescribe a lethal dosage of pills that must be self-administered by the patient. The goal of the law is to limit the patient's suffering.

54

Attempts to legalize assisted suicide have been made in numerous other states but have failed. Opposition has come from a broad spectrum of groups, including medical associations, disability rights organizations, faith-based groups, and civil rights organizations. As the United States population ages (the average life expectancy today is 78), more people die of chronic (long term) ailments contracted months or years before their deaths. Given this circumstance, patients will predictably seek, in greater numbers, their doctors' help in ending their lives. This will no doubt prompt in many states reconsideration of legalizing assisted suicide.

Application to HP Facts: Snape had several motivations for killing Dumbledore. One was to convince Voldemort and his followers of Snape's allegiance. Another was to relieve Dumbledore's physical deterioration and anticipated suffering. Unlike the definition of assisted suicide, Snape did not just aid or assist Dumbledore in ending his life; rather, Snape did the act that caused Dumbledore's death – using the Avada Kedavra Curse. Therefore, Snape would be guilty of not "just" assisted suicide, but rather murder. While both are serious felonies, murder is the higher level crime and could subject Snape to life in prison or, depending on the state, the death penalty, if convicted.

* * * * * * * * * * * * *

Other Areas of Law Implicated by These Facts
Death Penalty
Murder

CHAPTER 19

ASSAULT AND BATTERY – THE CRIME

Brazen, Berserk Bellatrix Beats Hermione

HP Facts: After being caught by Snatchers in the woods, Harry, Ron, and Hermione were taken to Voldemort's new headquarters, Malfoy Manor. Bellatrix Lestrange and other Death Eaters were there. Bellatrix was furious that Harry, Ron, and Hermione had the Sword of Gryffindor, believing they had stolen it from her vault at Gringotts Bank. After locking Harry, Ron, and others in the cellar, Bellatrix tortured Hermione for information about where she had obtained the sword. Hermione screamed repeatedly as Bellatrix used the Cruciatus Curse on her. (*DH–23*) Later, following Hermione's escape from Malfoy Manor, she recovered from the attack but, as she stood during Dobby's funeral, was "pale and unsteady on her feet." (*DH-24*)

Additional HP Facts: The Committee for the Disposal of Dangerous Creatures ruled that Buckbeak should be executed after he injured Draco Malfoy. Thereafter, Hermione confronted Draco, furious that he had exaggerated his injuries to the Committee. Hermione marched up to Draco and slapped him hard across his face using all her strength. She would have hit Draco again, but Ron stopped her. (*POA-15*)

Muggle Law: The crime of assault, which many states call battery, consists of intentionally causing physical injury. In numerous states, the requirement of an injury is satisfied if the victim suffers substantial pain but no other consequence. The crime is elevated and the potential jail time increased if a weapon is used or the victim suffers a serious, long-term injury, such as blindness in an eye. In situations where a person hits another but no injury results, the conduct may

56

consist of a lesser offense called, in some states, *harassment*. This wrong involves hitting, pushing or shoving someone with the intent to cause annoyance or alarm.

Application to HP Facts: Bellatrix's actions clearly constitute assault. She used her wand to administer substantial pain to Hermione, who repeatedly cried out in agony. The wand would be considered a weapon, increasing the seriousness of the crime and Bellatrix's potential sentence.

Concerning Hermione's slapping Draco, while she did intentionally hit him, we are not told if Draco suffered any injury. A slap customarily results in a momentary sting but not substantial pain or injury. Without one or the other, the crime of assault has not been committed. Hermione's actions would likely constitute harassment.

* * * * * * * * * * * * * *

Other Areas of Law Implicated by These Facts
Assault and Battery – The Torts
False Imprisonment
Kidnapping
Larceny
Robbery

CHAPTER 20

KIDNAPPING

Confounded Confinements

HP Facts: Bertha Jorkins, a Ministry employee at the Department of Magical Games and Sports, took a trip to Albania and never returned. Turns out, she was overpowered by Wormtail and taken to Voldemort where she was held captive because Voldemort wanted information from her to assist him in returning to power. Unfortunately, her confinement ended in her death. (*GOF-33*)

Additional HP Facts: Barty Crouch, Jr., with the help of Wormtail, overpowered Mad Eye Moody prior to the beginning of the school year. Crouch imprisoned Moody in a magical trunk for many months. (*GOF-35*)

Additional HP Facts: Voldemort needed information from Ollivander, the wand maker, to understand the *Priori Incantem* effect when Harry and Voldemort's wand connected. Voldemort also needed information regarding the Elder Wand. Additionally, because Luna's father was publishing in his magazine, the *Quibbler*, articles that were supportive of Harry and against Voldemort's Ministry agenda, Luna was taken off the Hogwarts Express by Death Eaters. Both Ollivander and Luna were held captive in the basement of Malfoy Manor. (*DH-23*)

Muggle Law: The crime of kidnapping is committed when a person restricts someone's freedom of movement against his will. Once kidnapped, the victim is not free to come and go but rather is restrained by the kidnapper.

Note: Although the name of the crime is "kidnapping," victims of the crime can be adults as well as youngsters.

Application to HP Facts: Voldemort and Wormtail are guilty of the crime of kidnapping for overpowering Bertha Jorkins and holding her against her will. Additionally, Barty Crouch, Jr., who subsequently impersonated Moody without detection for an entire school year, is also guilty of the crime of kidnapping for overpowering Moody and imprisoning him. Likewise, the Death Eaters kidnapped Luna and Ollivander.

* * * * * * * * * * * * *

Other Areas of Law Implicated by These Facts

Assault and Battery – The Crime
Assault and Battery – The Torts
Conspiracy
Death Penalty
False Imprisonment
Freedom of the Press
Identity Theft
Murder

CHAPTER 21

IDENTITY THEFT

Are You Me?

HP Facts: The story throughout *GOF* revolves around Barty Crouch, Jr. using Polyjuice Potion to impersonate and take the identity of Mad Eye Moody. But for this, Harry would not have competed in the Triwizard Tournament, which ultimately led to the re-birth of, and confrontation with, Lord Voldemort.

Additional HP Facts: Harry, Hermione, and Ron determined that a Horcrux was stored in Bellatrix Lestrange's vault at Gringott's Bank. With the help of Griphook, a former bank employee, they hatched a plan to gain access to the vault. To get past the goblin bank officials, Hermione took Polyjuice Potion to impersonate Bellatrix. (*DH-26*)

Muggle Law: Most states and the federal government have adopted a statute addressing identity theft. This crime occurs when someone uses your personal information – such as your name, credit card number, bank account number, or social security number – without your permission to fraudulently obtain a financial benefit. For example, the thief, armed with financial and personal information about you, opens a credit card account or a new cell phone account in your name, typically using the thief's address. The thief then makes purchases and does not pay the bills. You are unaware of this theft because the bills are mailed directly to the thief. Bye-bye good credit. Other scams include the thief's ordering checks on your bank account and using them to spend your money. Or the thief might take out a loan in your name and not make payments when due.

How is the thief able to get the necessary personal and financial information? There are numerous methods. They

60

include: rummaging through trash for bills and other papers containing personal information; pretending online to be a financial institution and asking for personal information; diverting your billing statements to another location by filling out a change-of-address form at the post office; and stealing your wallet or purse, which typically contains lots of identifying information.

Application to HP Facts: Concerning Barty Crouch, Jr., he took on the persona of Mad Eye Moody for the entire school year. In so doing, he impersonated Moody and stole his identity. Presumably, he was collecting Moody's salary from Hogwarts, and we know he was using Moody's personal possessions, including the magical eye and prosthetic leg, living quarters, and office.

Regarding Hermione's impersonation of Bellatrix, her objective was to gain access to Bellatrix's vault to steal the cup containing the Horcrux. Both of these circumstances constitute identity theft.

* * * * * * * * * * * * * *

Other Areas of Law Implicated by These Facts
Kidnapping
Larceny
Robbery
Trespass

CHAPTER 22

HATE CRIMES

Muffling Muggles

HP Facts: Following the final match of the Quidditch World Cup, the spectators returned to their campsites on the outskirts of the stadium. Later that night, Mr. Weasley woke Harry, Hermione, and the other Weasleys because screams were heard and people were running all about. A crowd of wizards, hooded and masked, were marching through the campsite. They had jinxed four Muggles who were levitated and floating above the crowd in midair, contorted into grotesque shapes. The Muggles were Mr. Roberts, the campsite manager, his wife, and their two small children. At one point, one of the marchers flipped Mrs. Roberts upside down exposing her underwear which she struggled to cover. Harry, Ron, and Hermione then ran into Draco Malfoy who gleefully explained that the hooded wizards were after Muggles. He threatened that if Hermione were not careful, she too would be showing off her underwear since she was a Mudblood. (*GOF-9*)

Additional HP Facts: Following the takeover of the Ministry of Magic by Voldemort and his Death Eaters, Harry, Ron, and Hermione went into hiding while they searched for Horcruxes. One night, Ron was able to tune *Potterwatch* in on the radio. For the first time in a long time, they were able to hear news about what was going on during their long seclusion. One of their friends, Lee Jordan, reported on the broadcast that a Muggle family of five was found dead in their home. He further stated that the Killing Curse was responsible and that "Muggle slaughter is becoming little more than a recreational sport under the new regime." (*DH-22*)

Muggle Law: The term "hate crime" refers to a criminal activity where the perpetrator targets specific victims because of their race, color, national origin, gender, religion, religious practices, age, disability, or sexual orientation. (Together, these categories are called "protected classes.") The most frequent motivation for hate crimes includes race, religion, skin color, and sexual orientation.

Forty-five states and the District of Columbia have adopted hate crime statutes. These laws generally fall into one of two categories: either they enhance the penalties for existing crimes when the motivation is prejudice, or they define specific bias-motivated acts that constitute a new crime distinct from conduct already defined as criminal but not motivated by bias.

The reason for separate treatment of hate crimes is that they inflict significant emotional harm on their victims and incite both community unrest and retaliatory crimes. The existence of hate crimes statutes makes a powerful statement that the states that impose them are intolerant of prejudice against the protected classes.

Application to HP Facts: The hooded wizards and Voldemort's followers targeted Muggles as victims of criminal conduct, not because of anything the Muggles did, but simply because of their status as Muggles. This equates to racial discrimination and would constitute a hate crime. The potential jail time, fines, and other penalties would appropriately increase due to the bias motivation for the crime.

* * * * * * * * * * * * * *

Other Areas of Law Implicated by These Facts
Assault and Battery - The Crime
Assault and Battery - The Torts
Criminal Mischief/Vandalism

Other Areas of Law Implicated by These Facts
(continued)
Equal Protection
Freedom of Speech
Freedom of the Press
Murder
Riot

CHAPTER 23

ENDANGERING THE WELFARE OF
AN INCOMPETENT PERSON

Basement Tales

HP Facts: When Albus and Aberforth Dumbledore's sister, Ariana, was six years old, she was attacked by three Muggle boys. She "was never the same again." Ariana's family hid her to ensure that she was not considered a threat to expose their world and break the International Statute of Secrecy. (*DH-28*) In Rita Skeeter's tell-all book entitled, *The Life and Lies of Albus Dumbledore*, questions were raised regarding the treatment and care of Ariana. These questions included whether Ariana had been mistreated by being imprisoned in the cellar of the Dumbledore home. (*DH–8,18*)

Muggle Law: Numerous states have a crime called endangering the welfare of an incompetent person. The crime is committed when someone causes injury to a person who is unable to care for herself because of a mental disease. A few states also include physically disabled people within the statute's protection. In some states, the crime is a misdemeanor and in others, a felony. Among the specific actions outlawed are inducing incompetent persons to participate in dangerous conduct, mistreating them resulting in injury, and engaging them in sexual activity. (A mentally incompetent person is unable, in the eyes of the law, to consent to sexual contact.)

Application to HP Facts: If Ariana had been locked in the cellar without oversight or care, this would likely constitute the crime of endangering the welfare of an incompetent person. If she had been confined in the cellar for long periods of time without food or monitoring, that would certainly constitute the crime.   The facts in the book concerning her care are not sufficiently detailed to determine whether the crime was committed.

* * * * * * * * * * * *

Other Areas of Law Implicated by These Facts
Assault and Battery - The Crime
Assault and Battery – The Torts

V.

CRIMES AGAINST PROPERTY

CHAPTER 24

LARCENY

Sticky Fingers

HP Facts: In two separate instances, Hermione and Barty Crouch Jr. each took ingredients for the Polyjuice Potion from Professor Snape's storage closet without his knowledge or consent. (*COS-11, GOF-27*)

Additional HP Facts: After Harry inherited Number Twelve Grimmauld Place and its contents from Sirius Black, Mundungus Fletcher helped himself to an assortment of objects, including a goblet that had the Black family crest on it. Always trying to make a buck and seldom doing it legally, Fletcher intended to sell the stolen items but Harry stopped him before any were sold. *(HBP-12)*

Additional HP Facts: Riddle stole some merchandise that had historical and sentimental value in the Wizarding world. Using a hex, he stole his grandfather's ring from his uncle, Morfin. *(HBP-17)* Riddle also filched from Hepzibah the cup that at one time belonged to Helga Hufflepuff and the locket that Salazar Slytherin had owned. *(HBP-20)*

Muggle Law: If someone takes your property without your permission and intends not to return it, that person has committed the crime of *larceny*. This is the legal word for stealing.

Application to HP Facts: In all three of the examples, the bandits have committed the crime of larceny. *Note:* Only someone with nerves of steel would steal from Snape.

Dear Diary

HP Facts: Harry kept Tom Riddle's diary in his trunk in the dormitory room at Hogwarts. One day, Harry discovered it missing. We later learn the culprit was none other than Ginny

Weasley; but when she took the book, she was under Riddle's total control and had no idea what she was doing. *(COS-14)*

Muggle Law: Larceny, like all crimes, requires two necessary components. The first is a wrongful act, and the second is a criminal mental state. The latter requirement usually means that the perpetrator intended to commit the crime. The absence of either component negates criminal liability.

Application to HP Facts: This circumstance presents a very interesting twist. Since Ginny was possessed by Riddle when she took the journal, she did not <u>intend</u> to take it. Rather, she was unwittingly carrying out Riddle's directives. Since Ginny lacked the criminal mental state, she would not be guilty of stealing. This is true even though she removed the diary without Harry's okay.

* * * * * * * * * * * * * *

Other Areas of Law Implicated by These Facts
Burglary
Trespass

CHAPTER 25

ROBBERY

Hands Up!

HP Facts: Tom Riddle took property from the other children at the orphanage. Professor Dumbledore stated that Riddle robbed the children to obtain their possessions. (*HBP-13,20*)

Muggle Law: Robbery is an aggressive form of larceny. It occurs when property is stolen from the victim by force. For example, a perpetrator approaches a person waiting for a bus, knocks him down, grabs his wallet, and runs. Factors that make the crime more serious include the use of a weapon and causing injury.

Application to HP Facts: If, in fact, Riddle used force, threats of force or threats of other aggressive conduct to take property from his orphan-mates, his crime would be robbery. If he stole the items from the others' rooms when they were out, the crime would be larceny and not robbery because the property would not have been taken from the victim's possession and not taken by force.

Give Me All Your Galleons!

HP Facts: Harry deduced that one of Voldemort's Horcruxes was being kept in the vault of the Lestrange family which was located at Gringotts Bank. Harry, Hermione, and Ron, with the help of the goblin Griphook, a former Gringotts bank employee, devised a plan to steal the cup that contained the Horcrux from the bank vault. In order to gain access to Gringotts and the vault, Harry used the Confundus Charm to confuse a bank guard and the Imperious Curse to control the bank employee who took them to the vault. Although the task was not easy, they were successful in stealing the cup and escaped on the back of the dragon guarding the vault. (*DH-26*)

Muggle Law: Bank robbery is a federal crime that is committed when the perpetrator takes money or property from a bank by using force against a teller or other bank employee responsible for the property's safekeeping.

Application to HP Facts: Harry used various spells to incapacitate several Gringotts bank employees in the process of taking the cup that housed the Horcrux from Bellatrix's vault. This would constitute bank robbery.

* * * * * * * * * * * * *

Other Areas of Law Implicated by These Facts
Assault and Battery – The Crime
Assault and Battery – The Torts
Bullying
Burglary
Identity Theft
Larceny

CHAPTER 26

UNAUTHORIZED USE OF A MOTOR VEHICLE

Joy Ride

HP Facts: The Dursleys' had imprisoned Harry by locking him in his room and putting steel bars on his windows. Unbeknownst to their parents, Ron, Fred, and George flew the enchanted Ford Angelina to the Dursleys' house to rescue Harry. To reach him, the Weasleys tied a rope around the window bars and pulled them from the house with the car. Fred and George then entered the Dursleys' house through the window, used a hairpin to pick the lock on the door to Harry's room, and then proceeded down the stairs to retrieve Harry's trunk. *(COS-3)* Later on, having missed the Hogwarts Express, Ron and Harry drove the car from the train station in London to Hogwarts where they crashed into the Whomping Willow. *(COS-5)*

Muggle Law: These facts constitute the crime of unauthorized use of a motor vehicle. The elements of this crime are (1) driving or riding in a car which belongs to someone else, and (2) knowing the owner has not given permission to drive the car. The crime also includes unauthorized use of a bus, motorcycle, snowmobile, plane, motorized boat, or truck.

Application to HP Facts: Had Mr. Wesley given permission for the boys to use the car, their actions would not amount to a crime. However, Mr. Weasley did not know that the car was anywhere but at the Burrow and had not given permission for its use. Since the brothers knew they did not have the okay to operate the Ford, they committed the crime of unauthorized use of a motor vehicle.

* * * * * * * * * * * * * *

Other Areas of Law Implicated by These Facts
Child Neglect and Abuse
Criminal Mischief/Vandalism
Negligence
Restrictions on Minors
Trespass

CHAPTER 27

TRESPASS

Shack Attack

HP Facts: When Harry reached the qualifying age for Hogwarts, owls flooded the Dursleys' house in an attempt to deliver Harry's invitation to attend the school. To get away from all of the letters and their winged carriers, Uncle Vernon took the family to a broken down shack on what appeared to be a large rock out in the middle of the sea. Professor Dumbledore, intent on making contact with Harry, sent Hagrid to the shack as the messenger. When Hagrid arrived, he knocked loudly several times but Uncle Vernon refused to open the door. Hagrid then beat down the door using such force that it came off its hinges and crashed to the ground. Uncle Vernon demanded that Hagrid leave as he was "breaking and entering." *(SS-3,4)*

Muggle Law: Trespass includes entering a building without permission of the owner or the person who lawfully occupies the building. For example, you cannot enter other people's houses unless they invite you in. If, however, a building is open to the public, such as a store during business hours, you are, of course, entitled to go in.

Trespass also includes remaining in a building after it closes. Suppose you are in J.C. Penney's at closing time. You hear on the loud speaker an announcement that the store is about to close. Rather than leave, you hide in the bathroom until all the salespeople have left. You are now remaining unlawfully, and therefore trespassing, even though when you entered the store you did so lawfully.

Application to HP Facts: Although the Dursleys did not own the shack, they apparently had the permission of the owner to occupy it at the time of Hagrid's arrival. Anyone entering the building without the Dursleys' permission would be trespassing. When Hagrid knocked down the door and entered, he was indeed trespassing.

Umbridge Would Take Umbrage if She Knew

HP Facts: Harry wanted very much to talk with Sirius. Yet all the mail and fireplaces in the castle were being guarded by Professor Umbridge to prevent just such a conversation. The only unguarded fireplace in the place was her own. Harry, being the daring guy that he is, conspired with Fred and George to create a diversion that would preoccupy Umbridge. While she was engaged trying to quell the commotion, Harry used the blade of his magical knife to pick the lock on her door. He entered, found her flu powder, and made glorious contact with Sirius and Lupin at Number Twelve Grimmauld Place. *(OOP-29)*

Muggle Law: Permission to enter a building does not necessarily include authorization to enter all parts of the building. A person can enter lawfully but still trespass if he goes to areas where permission to enter has not been given. If some space is marked "private," "keep out," or other similar term, entry is prohibited. For example, you might be in a store to shop and see a room or area marked "for employees only." Entry into that room or space is not allowed unless you are an employee. If you go in, you will be trespassing.

Application to HP Facts: Harry, of course, was entitled to be in the castle as a student at Hogwarts. His entry into Umbridge's office, however, was totally without the slightest bit of authority. His actions constituted trespassing.

* * * * * * * * * * * * * *

Other Areas of Law Implicated by These Facts
Aiding and Abetting
Criminal Mischief/Vandalism
Mail Abuse

CHAPTER 28

BURGLARY

Shredded Skin of a Boomslang

HP Facts: Harry, Ron, and Hermione believed that Draco Malfoy was the Heir of Slytherin and was plotting against Muggle-borns. Their best shot for verifying this belief was to disguise Harry and Ron as Crabbe and Goyle, an unlikely achievement but for the Polyjuice Potion. Hermione suggested breaking into Professor Snape's private storage closet to steal rare, but much-needed, ingredients for the potion, including boomslang skin. She later did steal the ingredients. (*COS-10,11*)

An Orderly Lawn

Additional HP Facts: While Harry was locked in his room and the Dursleys went off to claim their prize at the non-existent All-England Best Kept Suburban Lawn Competition (don't you just love the scene!), Harry heard a crash in the kitchen downstairs. "He sat bolt upright, listening intently . . .. Burglars he thought." In fact, the visitors were members of the Order of the Phoenix, including Mad-Eye Moody, Professor Lupin, Tonks, Kingsley Shacklebolt, Sturgis Podmore, and others. They had come to take Harry to the Order's headquarters. (*OOP-3*)

Muggle Law: The crime of burglary consists of trespass (entering or remaining unlawfully) with the addition that the intruder intends to commit a crime once inside the building. Thus, if the wrongdoer enters a neighbor's house while the neighbor is away, and the intruder's sole objective is to look around and see how his neighbor lives, this is trespass and not burglary. If, however, the perpetrator saw the neighbor bring home a new TV recently and the motive for entering the house

77

was to steal the television, the crime is burglary. This is true even if, for whatever reason, the perpetrator leaves without the TV. If, in fact, our burglar removes the TV and takes it home, he has committed both burglary and larceny.

Proving the necessary intent for burglary can be tricky. Usually the trespasser's actions once inside the building will evidence the intention. For example, if the intruder walks out with a television or piles merchandise near the door, it is fair to conclude that his intention in entering was to steal property.

Application to HP Facts: When Hermione entered Snape's storage area with the intention of taking the needed ingredients, she entered without permission and so committed burglary. If Snape had caught her before she was able to slip away and before she took the boomslang skin, the crime would still be burglary.

Concerning the second example, since Lupin and crew were not invited into the Dursleys' home, their entry constitutes trespass. They did not intend to commit a crime once inside so, contrary to Harry's thinking, they were not burglars. This is a good illustration of the distinction between trespass and burglary. The intent makes all the difference.

* * * * * * * * * * * * *

Other Areas of Law Implicated by These Facts
Identity Theft
Larceny
Trespass

CHAPTER 29

CRIMINAL MISCHIEF/VANDALISM

Gangbusters, Bathroom Hijinks and the Writing on the Wall

HP Facts: Harry's cousin Dudley is a member of a gang. The group vandalized the swings in a park. They also threw stones at passing cars. (*OOP-1*)

Additional HP Facts: *The Daily Prophet* reported that Willy Widdershins jinxed toilets so that they regurgitated. (*OOP-22*)

Additional HP Facts: While waiting to enter the Ministry of Magic building in London, Harry, Ron, and Hermione found themselves in an alleyway where there was a back door to an empty theatre. In order to gain entry, Hermione pointed her wand at the padlock on the heavily graffittied fire door "which burst open with a crash." (*DH-12*)

Muggle Law: Criminal mischief is the crime of intentionally causing damage to property. For example, if you slash a tire on someone's car, that would be criminal mischief. In some states the crime is called vandalism.

Application to HP Facts: Dudley and his fellow gang members intentionally caused injury to the park playground equipment by breaking the swings. They also threw stones at passing cars, likely causing damage to the vehicles. These acts constitute criminal mischief.

Concerning the toilets, once jinxed, they were unable to perform their function properly. The toilets were thereby damaged. Willy's actions, therefore, also constitute criminal mischief.

79

Regarding the fire door, words or drawings scribbled on a wall or door constitute graffiti and customarily diminish the value of the property. Some states include graffiti as part of their criminal mischief statute. Others have a specific crime called making graffiti.

* * * * * * * * * * * * *

Other Areas of Law Implicated by These Facts
Bullying
Freedom of the Press

CHAPTER 30

ARSON

Order Ordered Ostracized

HP Facts: After the takeover of the Ministry of Magic by Voldemort and his Death Eaters, Harry, Ron, and Hermione hid out at Number Twelve Grimmauld Place. Remus Lupin arrived and told the trio about how the Death Eaters had been "forcing their way into every Order-connected house in the country" searching for Harry. Lupin also told them how malicious and rough the Death Eaters had been and that they had burned down the house of Dedalus Diggle. (*DH-11*)

Muggle Law: The crime of arson consists of intentionally damaging a building or motor vehicle by starting a fire or causing an explosion. The seriousness of the crime is elevated when people are in the building or vehicle at the time of the fire and from the facts, the perpetrator should have known.

Application to HP Facts: The Death Eaters who burned Diggle's house would be guilty of arson. Had Dedalus been in the home at the time, his presence would have elevated the seriousness of the crime. Fortunately, he was not.

* * * * * * * * * * * * * *

Other Areas of Law Implicated by These Facts
Assault and Battery –The Crime
Assault and Battery – The Torts
Burglary
Trespass

CHAPTER 31

FORGERY

Who's John Hancock?

HP Facts: For eligible students (third year and older) to visit Hogsmead Village on select weekends, the students were required to have a parent or guardian sign a permission form. Harry was unable to get Uncle Vernon to sign his form. Harry was also unable to convince Cornelius Fudge or Professor McGonagall to sign it. Dean Thomas, "who was good with a quill," offered to forge Uncle Vernon's signature. Harry declined. He knew he would not get away with it since he had already told McGonagall that his uncle had not signed the form. (*POA-8*)

Additional HP Facts: For the Triwizard Tournament, students wishing to represent their school as champions and who are at least 17 years old, are invited to write their name on a piece of parchment and place it in the Goblet of Fire. Harry's name unexplainably came out as a Triwizard Champion despite his being underage and the fact he did not submit his name. We subsequently learn that Barty Crouch, Jr., posing as Moody, wrote Harry's name on parchment and placed it in the Goblet. (*GOF-17,35*)

Muggle Law: Signing another person's name without his knowledge or permission constitutes the crime of forgery provided the signer intended to deceive or injure another person.

Forgery is not limited to signing another person's name. It also includes making or altering a written document without permission with the intent to mislead someone else. For example, let's say you are playing bingo using two playing cards. On one card you are one number short of bingo (five called numbers in a row). On the other card, you have a number that would complete the bingo. If you cut out the number from the second card and attach it to the first card and then claim to be a winner, you have committed forgery.

Application to HP Facts: Had Dean signed Uncle Vernon's name, that would have been forgery since Dean did not have Harry's uncle's permission to sign his name.

Barty Crouch, Jr. was guilty of forgery for writing Harry's name on the parchment without Harry's okay. The Goblet believed that Harry volunteered to participate. Once selected, he had no choice but to participate. As intended by Crouch, his deception led to Harry's participation in the Tournament which led to Harry's capture and Voldemort's return.

* * * * * * * * * * * * * *

Other Areas of Law Implicated by These Facts
Freedom of Contract
Identity Theft
In Loco Parentis
Restrictions on Minors

VI.

CRIMINAL
BEHAVIOR -
MISCELLANEOUS

CHAPTER 32

LOITERING

Robed Idlers

HP Facts: In the beginning, before infant Harry was left at the Dursleys' doorstep, Mr. Dursley noticed on his way to work lots of people standing around dressed strangely in cloaks. Several huddled together whispering excitedly. (*SS-1*)

Muggle Law: The crime of loitering consists of remaining or wandering about in a public place for the purpose of committing a crime such as prostitution, using illegal drugs, or gambling. People have the right to linger in a public place for innocent purposes. If a person's reason for idling is merely to hang out and does not include doing anything illegal, that is permissible and does not constitute loitering. Thus, for example, you can socialize with friends in a park provided you do not block passersby, create a disturbance, or otherwise engage in outlawed behavior.

The crime of loitering also includes lingering in places where public access is restricted such as a school building or railroad tracks. Numerous states prohibit remaining in a public place being masked or otherwise disguised by unusual attire.

Application to HP Facts: Various wizards had gathered in and around London to celebrate Voldemort's downfall. Since they were not engaging in any illegal activity, their presence did not violate the loitering law. Further, although to the Muggle eye they were attired strangely, they were not wearing masks nor did their cloaks disguise their identity. Therefore, their unusual clothing would not render them guilty of loitering.

* * * * * * * * * * * * * *

Other Areas of Law Implicated by These Facts
Freedom of Assembly
Freedom of Speech

CHAPTER 33

DISTURBING THE PEACE/DISORDERLY CONDUCT

Fracas without Fracture

HP Facts: Harry, Hermione, her parents, and the Weasleys were shopping for school books at Flourish and Blotts in Diagon Alley. Unfortunately, they run into Lucias and Draco Malfoy. Lucias insulted Mr. Weasley, his family and the Grangers. In response, Mr. Weasley "threw himself" at Mr. Malfoy. A brawl ensued, knocking bookshelves over and causing the crowd to "stampede backwards." Fortunately Hagrid was close by and broke up the fight. (*COS-4*)

Muggle Law: Virtually every state has a law called either disorderly conduct or disturbing the peace. These statutes typically outlaw numerous types of unruly conduct that occur in a public place. Included among the prohibited behaviors are fighting, using vulgar language, unreasonable noise, and disrupting a group of people. Police typically rely on these statutes to keep the peace when a person is behaving in a disruptive manner.

Application to HP Facts: Mr. Weasley and Lucias were engaged in a fight in a public store. Their clash interfered with shoppers whose safety was threatened. The two men thus violated the disorderly conduct/disturbing the peace statute.

Note: The fact that Lucias initiated the encounter by demeaning and mean-spirited comments in no way justifies Mr. Weasley's reaction, nor relieves him from liability.

* * * * * * * * * * * * * *

Other Areas of Law Implicated by These Facts
Assault and Battery – The Crime
Assault and Battery – The Torts
Bullying
Defamation

CHAPTER 34

RIOT

Post-Quidditch Chaos

HP Facts: Following the final match at the Quidditch World Cup, the spectators returned to their campsites on the outskirts of the stadium. Later that night, Mr. Weasley woke Harry, Hermione, and the other Weasleys because screams were heard and people were running all about. A crowd of Death Eaters was marching through the campsite. They jinxed four Muggles who were levitated and floated above the crowd in midair, contorted into grotesque shapes. Then someone conjured the Dark Mark, which appeared ominously in the sky. (*GOF-9*)

Muggle Law: The crime of riot consists of tumultuous and violent conduct engaged in by several people that creates a risk of injury to the public. The number of participants required varies from state to state and ranges from three to seven. As the number of people taking part increases, so too does the seriousness of the crime.

Application to HP Facts: The Death Eaters made an appearance among the cavorting wizards with the intention of arousing fear. The appearance of a group of Voldemort's followers and their violent acts against the jinxed Muggles created a risk of injury to everyone at the campground. Their actions thus constituted the crime of riot.

* * * * * * * * * * * * * *

Other Areas of Law Implicated by These Facts
Freedom of Assembly
Assault and Battery – The Crime
Assault and Battery – The Torts
Disturbing the Peace/Disorderly Conduct
Hate Crimes

CHAPTER 35

MAIL ABUSE

All Shook Up

HP Facts: To his great surprise, there came a day while Harry lived with the Dursleys when he received a letter. It was addressed to him in the cupboard under the stairs. Harry did not think anyone but the Dursleys knew him and so he was very curious to know who sent it. As he attempted to read it, Uncle Vernon jerked the letter away. A fight for it ensued, which Harry lost. The next day, another letter arrived for Harry and again Uncle Vernon wrestled it away. Next day, three letters arrived prompting Uncle Vernon to nail closed the mail slot. The next day, 24 letters came, this time placed in the egg boxes delivered by the milkman. Aunt Petunia shredded them in the food processor. Next, 30 to 40 letters arrived down the chimney. Uncle Vernon ordered Harry out of the room without allowing him to read even one. To avoid the next onslaught, Uncle Vernon packed everyone into the car and headed for the coast. (*SS-3*)

Muggle Law: A federal crime called obstructing the mail forbids interfering with the delivery of mail to the intended recipient.

Application to HP Facts: Uncle Vernon intercepted mail addressed to Harry and refused to let him read it. Uncle Vernon would be guilty of the crime of obstructing the mail.

Boiling Mad

HP Facts: Rita Skeeter wrote various disparaging articles about Hermione in the *Daily Prophet* accusing Hermione of toying with the affections of both Harry and Viktor Krum. As a result, Hermione started receiving hate mail. After reading several letters, Hermione opened an envelope that contained yellowish-green liquid that got all over her hands. Ron thought that the liquid was undiluted bubotuber pus. Her hands erupted in large yellow boils that swelled her fingers and were very painful. She had no choice but to go to the hospital wing. (*GOF-28*)

Muggle Law: It is a federal crime to knowingly send hazardous materials through the mail.

Application to HP Facts: Since the letter was hate mail, the sender presumably intentionally included the dangerous pus, intending to cause Hermione injury. The sender's actions constitute a federal mail crime.

* * * * * * * * * * * * *

Other Areas of Law Implicated by These Facts
Assault and Battery – The Crime
Assault and Battery – The Torts
Defamation
Freedom of the Press

CHAPTER 36

CRUELTY TO ANIMALS

Ignoble Treatment of Gnomes, Tortoises and Dragons

HP Facts: Dudley was outraged that his parents gave Harry his second bedroom and had a temper tantrum. He hit his father with a stick, kicked his mother, and threw his tortoise through the greenhouse roof. (*SS-3*)

Additional HP Facts: Harry arrived at Ron's house for the first time in the enchanted flying car. While he was there, Mrs. Weasley asked Ron to de-gnome the garden. Harry, who had never done this before, offered to help. We learn that gnomes are small and leathery-looking creatures with large knobby bald heads that resemble potatoes and have horny little feet. When Ron caught one by the ankles, it yelled "gerrof me" several times. Ron then swung it around in circles like a lasso and threw it 20 feet. It landed with a thud. The goal, explained Ron, was to make them so dizzy they could not find their way back to their gnomeholes. Harry tried his hand at spinning and throwing the gnomes. "The air was soon thick with flying gnomes." In an effort to avoid this fate, one gnome bit Harry on the finger. (*COS-3*)

Additional HP Facts: Harry, Ron, Hermione, and Griphook the goblin descended to the Lestrange family vault at Gringotts Bank. As they approached the vault, a dragon roared and then retreated as they approached. Griphook explained that the dragon was taught to retreat when it heard the sound of the Clankers. Harry saw "vicious slash marks" across the dragon's face and surmised that it had been taught to fear hot swords when it heard the sound of the Clankers. (*DH-26*)

Muggle Law: Virtually all states have laws that outlaw animal cruelty and make it a crime. Typically, these statutes define animal cruelty as intentional conduct that causes unnecessary harm, pain or suffering to an animal. Also included is intentionally or negligently depriving an animal of food, drink, or needed veterinary care.

Application to HP Facts: An animal that is flung through a roof or on the ground is likely to be injured. Assuming the tortoise and gnomes were injured, the actions of Dudley, Ron, and Harry would constitute the crime of cruelty to animals. Likewise, inflicting substantial pain or injury on an animal to train it is illegal. Other less harmful behavior modification should be employed.

Concerning the dragon, if Harry's surmise about its training is correct, the trainer would be guilty of animal cruelty.

CHAPTER 37

ILLEGAL POSSESSION OF CULTURAL ARTIFACTS

More Malfoy Mischief; Cultural Conservation

HP Facts: Arthur Weasley worked for the Misuse of Muggle Artifacts Office at the Ministry of Magic. As part of his responsibilities, Mr. Weasley conducted raids on the homes of various wizards suspected of possessing illegal Wizarding artifacts that have dark magical qualities that could cause harm. Lucias Malfoy had a stash of such items. Concerned that his house would be raided and various illegal items found, he sold some to Borgin and Burkes in Knockturn Alley so he would not be caught with them. (*COS-4*)

Muggle Law: Countries and cultures have a strong interest in preserving their history as recorded in art and objects that inform about earlier civilizations. Such artifacts are appropriately maintained in museums and galleries. The inability to replace these items renders them high in value, a circumstance that attracts thieves. Many countries have laws that make theft or destruction of these articles or their removal from the country, a serious, international crime.

Artifacts that have been stolen include art work, hand-made objects indicative of a period in history, plant fossils, ceramic pots and kettles, statues, icons, jewelry, masks, documents, and items uncovered at archaeological sites.

Application to HP Facts: The artifacts Lucias had in his home were viewed by the Wizarding world as illegal to possess because of their dark magical qualities that could cause harm. Therefore, the presence of those items in Lucias' house constitutes a crime.

Hoard the Sword

HP Facts: Following the death of Professor Dumbledore, Minister of Magic Rufus Scrimgeour went to the Burrow to speak with Harry, Ron, and Hermione about Dumbledore's will. In his will, Professor Dumbledore bequeathed to Ron the Deluminator; to Hermione the book, *The Tales of Beedle the Bard;* and to Harry, the first Snitch that he caught in his very first Quidditch match and the Sword of Gryffindor. However, Scrimgeour refused to give Harry the sword stating, "the sword of Godric Gryffindor is an important historical artifact" and, therefore, Harry is not entitled to it. (*DH-7*)

Muggle Law: People can designate in their will whom they want to receive property they own, including cultural artifacts, after their death. While the government might like to own a particular artifact, such as the Sword, it could become the owner only by buying it or by the owner's designating the government as the beneficiary in a will.

If a person dies in possession of property he does not own, he cannot legally give it away in his will. Instead, the true owner is entitled to it. We have seen that cultural artifacts are quite valuable and often stolen. If a person possesses stolen artifacts at the time of his death, he cannot legally give them away in his will.

Application to HP Facts: If Dumbledore were the true owner of the Sword, he was entitled to give it to anyone he chose, and the Ministry would be violating the law by withholding it from Harry. This would be true even though the Sword was a valuable cultural artifact. On the other hand, if someone other than Dumbledore were the true owner, Harry would not be entitled to the Sword even though Dumbledore wanted Harry to have it.

* * * * * * * * * * * * * *

Other Areas of Law Implicated by These Facts
Will and Inheritance
Search and Seizure

CHAPTER 38

ILLEGAL POSSESSION OF DRUGS

A Seedy Transaction

HP Facts: Fred and George Weasley were experimenting with various substances, hoping to create new products for their joke shop. One of their suppliers of materials was Mundungus Fletcher, a shady character. While at the headquarters of the Order of the Phoenix at Number Twelve Grimmauld Place, Mundungus sold Fred and George Venomous Tentacle seeds for ten Galleons. Fred and George had been having trouble obtaining these seeds as they are a "Class C Non-Tradable Substance." (*OOP–9*)

Muggle Law: It is a crime to knowingly possess or sell certain drugs, which are called *controlled substances.* Among controlled substances are cocaine, heroin, stimulants, hallucinogens, concentrated cannabis, and more. Sale or possession of these drugs is viewed very seriously by most states and subjects the wrongdoer to many years in jail. Marijuana is illegal to possess or sell, although it is a less serious crime.

Application to HP Facts: Given that Venomous Tentacle seeds are a Nontradable Substance in the Wizarding world, they would presumably be a controlled substance in the Muggle world. As such, Mundungus would be guilty of a crime for selling them, and the twins would be guilty of illegal possession.

* * * * * * * * * * * * *

Other Areas of Law Implicated by These Facts
Legal Tender

97

CHAPTER 39

GAMBLING

Luck of the Irish

HP Facts: At the Quidditch World Cup, Fred and George Weasley bet Ludo Bagman all of their savings plus a fake wand that Ireland would win the Tournament, but Viktor Krum from the Bulgarian team would get the snitch. Luckily, the Weasleys won the bet. Unluckily, Bagman paid them with leprechaun gold which vanished by the next morning. (*GOF-8,37*)

Additional HP Facts: Bagman bet on Harry to win the Triwizard Tournament. (*GOF-37*)

Muggle Law: Gambling consists of wagering (risking) money or something else of value on a predicted outcome of an event with the hope of winning something, usually money, if the predicted result occurs. An example would be betting money on a particular team to win a baseball game or on specified numbers being drawn in a lottery. In most states, gambling is illegal. Approximately half of the states carve out an exception permitting social betting. This is gambling where all the money wagered is paid to the winner; none is retained by the game's organizer. What is prohibited in these states are gambling operations in which the organizer keeps a portion of the money bet.

Some gambling-related conduct that is illegal in most states has been legalized in some states. For example, Las Vegas, Nevada, is famous as the "gambling capital of the world." Its laws allow certain licensed businesses to profit from hosting gambling activities. The state is home to many casinos which offer games of chance to eager gamblers including black jack, roulette, craps, and numerous versions of poker. Other cities that have legalized some forms of gambling include Atlantic

City, New Jersey, and Tunica, Mississippi, as have numerous Native American tribes. Likewise, many states have legalized lotteries, such as Mega Millions and Powerball, which are games in which people bet a sum of money and attempt to predict which five or six numbers will be randomly drawn from a set of many numbers.

Application to HP Facts: The bet between the Weasley twins and Ludo Bagman would not be illegal in many states because all the money gambled was to be paid to the winner. If, however, someone were running a gambling operation during the Triwizard Tournament, accepting bets from numerous people, pocketing a portion of the money wagered, and paying the balance to the winner, the gambling scheme would constitute criminal activity.

* * * * * * * * * * * * *

Other Areas of Law Implicated by These Facts
Fraud
Larceny
Restrictions on Minors

CHAPTER 40

FORTUNE TELLING

Trelawney – Treasure or Treacherous?

HP Facts: In their third year at Hogwarts, Harry, Ron, and Hermione took a Divination class taught by Professor Trelawney, a rather eccentric teacher. She taught that Divination is a gift that allows those who possess it to "penetrate the veiled mysteries of the future." She told the class that they would be studying basic methods of Divination including reading tea leaves, palmistry, fire omens, and crystal ball gazing. (*POA-6*) Later, Harry witnessed Trelawney having a vision that foretold of Voldemort's servant Wormtail's rejoining his master who would rise again. (*POA–16*)

Muggle Law: Fortune telling means forecasting the future. In most states, fortune telling is legal. These states leave it to consumers to decide if they wish to spend their money on this unproven activity. Several states and some cities recognize that people do not have the ability to read the future with any reasonable degree of accuracy, and so they outlaw the practice of charging a fee for fortune telling. These states and municipalities consider fortune telling a form of fraud. The types of predictions they prohibit include reading palms, tarot cards, tea leaves, as well as crystal-ball gazing, and use of all other similar devices. In states where fortune telling is outlawed, it is permitted as part of a show or exhibition solely for the purpose of entertainment or amusement.

Application to HP Facts: Even those states and cities that prohibit charging a fee for fortune telling do not outlaw the subject's being taught. Therefore, neither Hogwarts nor

Trelawney would be subject to prosecution for teaching fortune telling. If Trelawney started a business of fortune telling and charged a fee for her services, she could be prosecuted in those locales where fortune telling is a crime.

CHAPTER 41

ESCAPE

Adios Azkaban

HP Facts: While riding The Knight Bus, Harry read an article in the *Daily Prophet* about Sirius Black. Harry then talked to the bus driver Stan Shunpike about Black's being at large after escaping from Azkaban Prison. Harry learned that Black was in prison for killing a dozen Muggles. (*POA-3*)

Additional HP Facts: Barty Crouch, Jr. was sent to Azkaban for his role in the capture and torture of Neville Longbottom's parents. Crouch escaped from Azkaban with the help of his parents. Crouch escaped from Azkaban with the help of his parents. He was able to get away by switching identities with his mother who took Polyjuice Potion to become Crouch, while Crouch took the Potion to pass as his mother. (*GOF-35*)

Muggle Law: The justice system is entitled to punish a wrongdoer. A component of a sentence can be jail time. The wrongdoer must pay the debt to society by completing his prison term. Attempts to avoid part of the sentence by breaking out of prison early constitutes the crime of escape and will likely result, in a longer sentence. The more serious the crime that resulted in the jail term, the more serious is the crime of escape. For example, escaping from a prison term imposed for robbery is a more serious crime than escaping from a jail sentence for stealing a small amount of merchandise.

Application to HP Facts: Sirius Black's unauthorized departure from Azkaban constitutes the crime of escape. He had been serving a sentence for murder, the most serious of crimes. His flight from prison would thus be the highest degree of the crime of escape.

Crouch's unauthorized, but clever, exit from Azkaban also constitutes the crime of escape. He was in the prison for a serious crime – assault causing permanent injury – and so the degree of escape he committed is high.

* * * * * * * * * * * * *

Other Areas of Law Implicated by These Facts
Aiding and Abetting
Identity Theft
Murder
Sentencing

CHAPTER 42

HINDERING PROSECUTION

A Friend in Need Can Lead You to Jail

HP Facts: As Hogwarts students, Remus Lupin and Sirius Black were friends. Several times following Black's escape from Azkaban Prison, Professor Snape mistakenly suspected that Professor Lupin had been helping Black gain unauthorized access to the school. Snape alludes to this in a conversation with Dumbledore after Black snuck into Hogwarts by slashing the Fat Lady's portrait. *(POA-9)*

Muggle Law: A person commits the crime of hindering prosecution if he (1) intends to obstruct the apprehension or prosecution of another, and (2) he "harbors or conceals" from law enforcement officials a person he knows or believes has committed a crime or is being sought by police for the commission of a crime. Hindering prosecution is also committed if, with the referenced intent, a person provides the fugitive with money, transportation, or a weapon, all of which would come in handy to someone seeking to avoid detection.

Application to HP Facts: If Snape had been correct and Lupin had been aiding Black to hide from authorities, Lupin would be guilty of the crime of hindering prosecution.

Two Faces Have I

HP Facts: Mr. and Mrs. Crouch helped their son escape from Azkaban. Barty Jr. used Polyjuice Potion to appear as his mother and walked out of prison without detection. Barty, Jr. was hidden at the Crouch home with the assistance of Mr. Crouch and Winky the house elf. *(GOF-35)*

Muggle Law: The crime of hindering prosecution includes aiding a prisoner in the use of a disguise or deception to prevent discovery by the police.

Application to HP Facts: Mr. and Mrs. Crouch used deception – the Polyjuice Potion – to prevent the authorities from discovering that Barty Crouch, Jr. left Azkaban. This assistance constitutes hindering prosecution. His father also hindered prosecution in an additional way by concealing his son in the Crouch home, thereby frustrating the Ministry's attempts to find Barty Jr. and return him to prison.

* * * * * * * * * * * * *

Other Areas of Law Implicated by These Facts
Aiding and Abetting
Escape
Identity Theft
Restrictions on Minors

CHAPTER 43

AIDING AND ABETTING

One if by Cabinet, Two if by Floo

HP Facts: Harry was disturbed by what he saw in the Pensieve as "Snape's Worst Memory." Harry's father James, who was 15 at the time, appeared to have bullied and humiliated Snape. This partially explained why Snape hated Harry's father and probably Harry as well. Harry needed to better understand what he had just seen and knew that Sirius could help him. The only way for Harry to converse with Sirius, who was at Twelve Grimmauld Place, was via the fireplace. However, Professor Umbridge had blocked communications through all fireplaces at Hogwarts except the one in her office. Access by students was strictly forbidden. Fred and George to the rescue! They diverted Umbridge's attention by conjuring a swamp that filled a corridor on the fifth floor. While she was busy tending to the mess, Harry gained entry to Umbridge's office by picking the lock with the help of a magical knife that Sirius had given him. (OOP-*28,32*)

Additional HP Facts: Voldemort's plan to infiltrate Hogwarts with Death Eaters was complicated by security measures Professor Dumbledore had put in place to protect the castle and its students. Voldemort enlisted the help of Draco Malfoy. Draco knew there was a broken Vanishing Cabinet in the Room of Requirement that connected with a Vanishing Cabinet at Borgin and Burkes in Knockturn Alley. Draco realized that if he could repair the cabinet at Hogwarts, it would create a pathway into the castle that the Death Eaters could use free from all of Dumbledore's protective measures. Draco spent much of his time during his sixth year at school repairing the cabinet. He was ultimately successful, enabling the Death Eaters to enter the castle, causing much havoc. Their presence led to the death of Dumbledore, the attack on Bill Weasley, and other injuries and damage at Hogwarts. (*HBP-27*)

Muggle Law: Anyone who intentionally participates in a crime or helps a criminal before or after the commission of the crime may be held responsible for it, depending on the circumstances. One's participation can vary in involvement and degree. The primary actor is called the *principal*. One who assists the principal is customarily referred to as an *accomplice* (sometimes called an accessory). A few states recognize that assistance in a crime is of varying degrees. A person whose assistance is of a lesser degree is identified in these states as a *facilitator*. The difference between an accomplice and a facilitator is based entirely on the participant's intent and not upon his actions. Thus, the difference is not always easy to recognize. Further information about each follows.

An accomplice is a person who both assists the principal in committing the crime and shares the principal's criminal intent that the crime be committed. An accomplice is viewed in law as equally guilty as the principal and faces the same possible sentence.

In contrast, a facilitator is someone who gives aid to the principal knowing his assistance will be used by the principal in the commission of a crime, but the facilitator does not intend to commit the crime. His intent is limited to assisting the principal. A facilitator is liable for a lower level crime than the one committed by the principal.

Application to HP Facts: Draco was an accomplice. He intended to enable the Death Eaters to enter Hogwarts (this would be the crime of trespass). Draco played an active role in securing their unauthorized entry. Had Voldemort been prosecuted criminally, Draco, as an accomplice would be as equally liable as the Death Eaters.

Fred and George, however, played a lesser role in the trespass of Umbridge's office. Their goal was to assist Harry in making contact with Sirius. They did not themselves intend to enter Umbridge's office or speak with Sirius. Therefore, they were facilitators and not accomplices. Had Harry been prosecuted criminally, the twins could face liability for a lesser charge.

* * * * * * * * * * * * *

Other Areas of Law Implicate by These Facts

Bullying
Conspiracy
Criminal Mischief/Vandalism
Trespass

CHAPTER 44

CONSPIRACY

Powerful Plotters

HP Facts: Harry learns from Barty Crouch, Jr., who posed as Professor Moody, how Harry's name was put in the Goblet of Fire for the Triwizard Tournament. Voldemort, Wormtail and Crouch together planned and submitted Harry's name. This enabled the plotters to arrange Harry's victory and his transport to the graveyard where he became an unwilling participant in the resurrection of You-Know-Who. (*GOF-35*)

Additional HP Facts: At the very beginning of *Deathly Hallows*, Voldemort and various Death Eaters were sitting at a long table discussing plans for Harry's kidnapping and Voldemort's takeover of the Ministry of Magic. Yaxley, one of the Death Eaters and a high-ranking Ministry employee, reported that in furtherance of the plan, he had put the Imperius Curse on Pius Thickness, the Head of the Department of Magical Law Enforcement. Thickness was thus under Voldemort's control. Yaxley advised Voldemort that, with Thickness under their control, it would be easier to overtake others at the Ministry and overthrow the Minister of Magic, Rufus Scrimgeour. (*DH-1*) Soon after, the Death Eaters attempted to capture Harry after he left the Dursleys' house. (*DH-4*)

Muggle Law: Conspiracy is a crime that occurs when two or more people agree to commit and thereafter engage in a criminal act in furtherance of that crime. For example, two people may decide to jointly rob a bank. One could enter the bank and show a gun to a teller while the other might subdue would-be rescuers or act as a lookout to prevent detection. The bank robbery is one crime. The separate crime of conspiracy consists of two elements (1) the agreement to jointly commit

109

the robbery, and (2) engaging in conduct that advances the crime.

Application to HP Facts: Crouch, Voldemort, and Wormtail together schemed to put Harry in harm's way. They intended him to confront Voldemort and hoped the encounter would lead to Harry's death or serious injury. Their joint plan to murder or injure plus the act of putting Harry's name in the Goblet of Fire constitutes conspiracy. If Harry had actually been killed or hurt, the conspirators would also have been liable for murder or assault.

Similarly, Voldemort and the Death Eaters planned to take over the Ministry by force and kidnap Harry. To effectuate this plan, Yaxley put the Imperious Curse on Thickness and an attempt was made to capture Harry. The joint planning to overtake the Ministry and to capture Harry, plus the actions taken to make their plan a reality, constitute the crime of conspiracy.

* * * * * * * * * * * * *

Other Areas of Law Implicated by These Facts
Freedom of Contract
Forgery
Government
Kidnapping
Murder

CHAPTER 45

MISCONDUCT OF PUBLIC OFFICIALS

Sign It Or Else

HP Facts: When the heir of Slytherin started attacking Muggle-borns, Lucias Malfoy presented Professor Dumbledore an Order of Suspension from his position as Headmaster of Hogwarts. Malfoy told Dumbledore that it had been signed by all 12 members of the board of governors. After Dumbledore was later reinstated, he told Lucias that several of the governors told him that the only reason they signed the Order of Suspension was because Lucias had threatened to curse their families. (*COS-14,18*)

Additional HP Facts: Harry, Ron, and Hermione believed that the locket they had previously seen at Number Twelve Grimmauld Place was, in fact, one of Voldemort's Horcruxes. They learn from Kreacher that Mundungus Fletcher had taken many things from Sirius' house, including the locket. When Harry confronted Mundungus about this, Mundungus told Harry that he no longer had the locket and that a "Ministry hag" (who Harry, Ron and Hermione surmised was Dolores Umbridge) took it from him. Umbridge asked Mundungus if he had a "license for trading in magical artifacts," and when he said no, she responded that if he would give her the locket, she would let him off this time. (*DH-11*)

Muggle Law: The crime of official misconduct involves a government employee who commits an act that constitutes the unauthorized exercise of his official functions.

Application to HP Facts: We know that cursing anyone in the Wizarding world is nasty business. Lucias was known to be ruthless, so his threats likely cowered some of the other governors into compliance with his wishes. By seeking

111

complicity in an unjustified suspension of Dumbledore, Lucias' actions constituted official misconduct.

Lucias, in his capacity as a governor of Hogwarts, has a duty to supervise the headmaster and, where appropriate, discipline and even suspend him. However, even if Dumbledore's suspension were warranted – which is far from the actual facts – the proper method for determining the appropriate discipline is a vote by the governors in which each evaluates the facts and makes an informed judgment about the suitable action. Securing votes for Lucias' position by threatening the governing board is an unauthorized exercise of Lucias' role as a governor and constitutes official misconduct.

Concerning Umbridge and the locket, she, too, misused her authority. When people engage in pursuits that require a license and they do not have the license, the proper disciplinary procedure is for a police officer or other law enforcement official to issue a *citation,* which is a document directing the unlicensed violator to appear in court to address the license issue. A public official who extracts a personal benefit in exchange for granting an exemption from prosecution, as Umbridge did, commits the crime of official misconduct.

* * * * * * * * * * * * *

Other Areas of Law Implicated by These Facts
Larceny
School Board

CHAPTER 46

SELF-DEFENSE AND DEFENSE OF OTHERS

Curses

HP Facts: Harry and Draco Malfoy had an altercation in Moaning Myrtle's bathroom after Harry overheard Draco crying to Myrtle. He was revealing fears that he would not be able to carry out Voldemort's plan, and Voldemort would kill him. Harry and Draco unsuccessfully attempted to curse each other. Draco was about to use the unforgivable Cruciatus Curse, but Harry beat him to the punch and used the Sectumsempra Curse that he had learned from the Half Blood Prince's potions textbook. As a result, Draco was cut on his face and chest as if he had been slashed with a sword and blood spewed out. Fortunately for Draco (and Harry), Professor Snape appeared almost immediately and applied a curing counter curse. He then took Draco to the hospital wing. (*HBP– 24*)

Muggle Law: A person is entitled to defend himself against an attack. This means the victim of the attack can legally use force against the aggressor. However, the amount of force permitted is limited. A person can use only that amount of force as is reasonably necessary to protect himself and repel the attack. If more force is used, the defender may face liability.

Application to HP Facts: Draco was in the process of casting an unforgivable curse against Harry – the Cruciatus Curse. Harry, in self-defense, was entitled to use a degree of force necessary to quell the attack. The Sectumsempra Curse sufficiently debilitated Draco so that he stopped his cursing against Harry. Whether or not Harry responded too aggressively depends on whether his use of the Sectumsempra Curse was reasonably necessary to repel the force Draco was using against him. If Harry overreacted, he could face liability

113

for battery. The more likely circumstance is that a powerful curse was necessary to neutralize Draco's intended Cruciatus Curse. If so, Harry's response was reasonable, and he can utilize the defense of self-defense to avoid liability.

Sock It to Me

HP Facts: Harry removed one of his dirty socks and stuffed it in Tom Riddle's diary. He then caught up with Lucias Malfoy and forced the smelly sock into Lucias' hand. Lucias, angry and annoyed, flung it aside. Dobby the house elf caught it. Because his master had "given" Dobby an article of clothing, Dobby was set free. Lucias, who was infuriated by this turn of events, lunged at Harry. Dobby used magic to protect Harry causing Lucias to be thrown backwards, crashing down the steps to the landing below. (*COS-18*)

Muggle Law: The right to defend against an invader includes not just the right to protect one's self but also another person.

Application to HP Facts: Given the imminent attack by Lucias against Harry, Dobby was justified in using the amount of force necessary to ward off the attack. This is true even though Harry, and not Dobby, was Lucias' target.

* * * * * * * * * * * * *

Other Areas of Law Implicated by These Facts
Assault and Battery – The Crime
Assault and Battery – The Torts

CHAPTER 47

INSANITY DEFENSE

Sister Dearest

HP Facts: Ariana was the sister of Albus and Aberforth Dumbledore. When she was six years old, she was attacked by three Muggle boys, after which was "was never right again." When Ariana was age 14, "she had one of her rages," and Ariana's mother was accidentally killed. (*DH-28*)

Muggle Law: *Insanity Defense.* The term *insanity defense* refers to an argument made by a defendant that he should not be held criminally responsible for breaking the law because he was mentally ill at the time he committed the crime. If the defendant proves that he was in fact insane, in most states, he is entitled to a finding of not guilty by reason of insanity. In some states, he will be found guilty but mentally ill. The legal definition of insanity used in this context is different than the use by psychiatrists. While the meaning varies somewhat from state to state, most states use a variation of the following: A person is insane and not criminally responsible if, due to a mental disease or defect, he is unable to appreciate the nature and consequences of his actions or that his actions are wrong.

Some states use an alternative rule called the irresistible-impulse test. This rule holds that a person is insane if he were unable to resist the urge to commit the criminal act because mental disease destroyed his self-control and ability to choose his actions. Both tests are difficult to apply. In a case where a defendant asserts the insanity defense, both the defendant and the prosecution each customarily hire a psychiatrist to interview the defendant and testify as an expert witness concerning the defendant's mental state.

Customarily, a defendant found to be insane at the time of the crime is placed in a mental health facility until his doctors determine that he is not a threat to others.

Age of Criminal Responsibility. A young person is not criminally responsible for his actions until he reaches an age of relative maturity. Until that time, a child lacks the judgment that comes only with age and experience and so is exempt from the adult system of criminal prosecution and punishment. The age when a child can be held responsible is determined by each state so consistency is lacking. An exception exists in some states for younger violators who commit murder or other violent felonies; they can be prosecuted as an adult.

Although criminal liability begins in late teen years, the law recognizes that the process of maturing is not then complete. Thus, in many states the criminal record of a late teen may be *sealed*, meaning that a potential employer will not learn about his criminal actions. In this way, some criminal activity that resulted from immaturity will not handicap the young person's future.

In most states, cases involving underage wrongdoers will be heard in family court rather than adult criminal court. In family court, the emphasis is less on punishment and more on treatment and care.

Application to HP Facts: The story does not give us enough facts about the circumstances of Dumbledore's mother's death or Ariana's mental condition to know if Ariana fits either definition of insanity. We are, however, given enough information to recognize that, if Ariana is prosecuted for her mother's murder, Ariana's attorney should investigate the possibility of an insanity defense. Likewise, the law relevant to age of criminal responsibility should be reviewed to determine if Ariana's case belongs in family court.

116

* * * * * * * * * * * * *

Other Areas of Law Implicated by These Facts
Assault and Battery – The Crime
Assault and Battery – The Torts
Restrictions on Minors

CHAPTER 48

JUSTIFICATION

Deathly Kiss

HP Facts: Harry and his cousin Dudley were attacked by two dementors in an alleyway in Little Whinging. One of the dementors was about to perform the "Kiss" on Dudley which would have sucked out his soul causing a fate considered, in the Wizarding world, worse than death. Harry used his wand to conjure a Patronus that drove the dementors away before either Dudley or he was harmed. (*OOP-1*) Harry was subsequently required to attend a disciplinary hearing at the Ministry of Magic where he was accused of violating two laws: (1) the Decree for the Reasonable Restriction of Underage Sorcery (the "Decree") for using magic outside of Hogwarts while not yet 17, and (2) the International Statute of Secrecy for performing magic in front of a Muggle. In Harry's defense, Professor Dumbledore pointed out that clause seven of the Decree provides that magic may be used in front of a Muggle "in exceptional circumstances" including when the life of the witch or wizard or Muggle present is at risk. (*OOP-8*)

Muggle Law: The law recognizes that, while certain conduct may be criminal, in an emergency, that same behavior may be both useful and advisable. The law thus recognizes a defense to a criminal charge called *justification,* which is very similar to clause seven of the Decree. The defense applies where the following four circumstances exist: (1) an emergency situation occurred; (2) someone commits criminal conduct during the emergency; (3) the crisis happened through no fault of the wrongdoer; and (4) the commission of the crime prevented a more serious injury than was caused by the criminal act committed.

Application to HP Facts: Harry's use of magic in the alleyway and in the presence of Dudley likely saved two souls that day – Dudley's and Harry's.   The performance of the dementor's Kiss would cause much greater injury than occurred from Harry's violation of the rule against use of magic away from Hogwarts or from a Muggle's witnessing the use of magic.   Harry would thus be able to use the defense of justification to avoid liability for his transgression.

* * * * * * * * * * * * *

Other Law Implicated by These Facts
Due Process for Students at Suspension Hearings
Notice and Opportunity to be Heard
Right to an Attorney
Self-Defense and Defense of Others

CHAPTER 49

EAVESDROPPING AND WIRETAPPING

Do Your Ears Hang Low? Do They Wobble To and Fro?

HP Facts: Following Harry's initial arrival at Number Twelve Grimmauld Place, he learned that the house was the secret headquarters for the Order of the Phoenix. Mrs. Weasley would not allow her children or Harry and Hermione to participate in Order meetings. To listen in, nonetheless, the mischievous Fred and George used one of their inventions, Extendable Ears. (*OOP-4*)

Additional HP Facts: Throughout *Goblet of Fire*, Hermione could not understand how Rita Skeeter was able to obtain information from private conversations for *Daily Prophet* articles when Rita was nowhere in sight. Once Hermione figured out that Rita was an unregistered Animagus and could transform herself into a beetle, it all made sense. As a small bug, Rita had been listening in unnoticed on private conversations. (*GOF-37*)

Muggle Law: Eavesdropping is a crime that recognizes the privacy of conversations. It outlaws the use of a device to overhear when people engaged in discussions would reasonably expect their comments to be private. Additionally, in some states, a crime exists that is called possession of an eavesdropping device. It prohibits possession of a mechanism used to listen in on others' conversations with the intent to use it to eavesdrop.

Application to HP Facts: Fred and George would be guilty of eavesdropping for using the Extendable Ears to decipher the conversation occurring in the kitchen. Additionally, mere possession of the Extendable Ears with the intent to use it for listening to the Order's private conversations constitutes in some states the additional crime of possession of an eavesdropping device.

Rita Skeeter's transformation to a beetle does not, of course, have a direct correlation to the Muggle world. Her use of a bug's agility to access otherwise unreachable places to facilitate eavesdropping would violate the law.

Voldemort Verboten

HP Facts: To track and capture those who opposed Voldemort, a "taboo" on his name was created. It identified the location of anyone with the audacity to say the name. Such a person was assumed to oppose Voldemort, such as members of the Order of the Phoenix. The result was easy capture by Voldemort's supporters. (*DH-20*) Unfortunately, Harry accidentally slipped and spoke Voldemort's name. Instantly, Harry, Ron, and Hermione were located, surrounded, and captured by Snatchers. (*DH–22,23*)

Muggle Law: In limited circumstances, law enforcement officers, such as police, are permitted to listen to and record people's private conversations. To do so requires an *eavesdropping warrant.* This is an order issued by a judge authorizing the interception of a conversation. Before a judge will issue the warrant, police officers must prove that they have reasonable cause to believe that the person whose conversations the police want to hear is committing a serious felony. Once the warrant is issued, police will often use a listening device called a "bug" to overhear the discussion. The bug is placed in an area where desired conversations are expected to occur and transmits the conversations to the police located elsewhere.

Application to HP Facts: The jinx on Voldemort's name enabled the Snatchers to overhear whenever someone said the name. If the Snatchers were engaged in law enforcement for the Ministry, they should have had a warrant. Since they did not, they would be in violation of the restrictions on eavesdropping. As a consequence, any evidence obtained from the intercepted conversations may not be usable at trial.

* * * * * * * * * * * * *

Other Areas Implicated by These Facts
Bounty Hunters
False Imprisonment
Kidnapping
Search and Seizure

VII.

RIGHTS WHEN CHARGED WITH A CRIME (CONSTITUTIONAL LAW, PART I)

CHAPTER 50

INVESTIGATIONS

The Facts, Please

HP Facts: Fifty years before Harry was born, Tom Riddle's father and grandparents were found dead in their home in Little Hangleton. The police found that the door to the house had not been forced nor were any of the windows broken. However, there had been a spare key hanging in the gardener's cottage for years. The Riddles' gardener, Frank Bryce, was arrested for the crime. Frank told the police that he was innocent and that he had seen a teenage boy near the house on the day of the Riddles' death. In furtherance of the investigation, a team of doctors examined the Riddles' bodies but were unable to figure out how they died. Without proof of who or what caused their deaths, the police had no choice but to release Frank. (*GOF-1*)

Additional HP Facts: Harry was put on trial before the Wizengamot for using magic to repel the dementors that attacked Dudley and him near the Dursleys' home. Professor Dumbledore offered evidence proving that the dementor attack did, in fact, occur and argued that Harry had the right to use magic under this emergency situation. Professor Umbridge retorted a dementor attack in Little Whinging was not possible because dementors are under Ministry control. Conceding nothing, Dumbledore responded that the Ministry should conduct a full investigation as to why the dementors left Azkaban Prison and attacked Harry and his cousin without authorization. (*OOP-8*)

Muggle Law: An investigation is the process of inquiring into circumstances where facts are unclear or in dispute. The purpose of an investigation is to uncover the truth. Investigations are usually done by police or government officials called (not surprisingly) investigators. Often, an investigation is done because a crime has been committed but the identity of the perpetrator has not yet been determined.

Assume, for example, that a store owner was robbed but the wrongdoer has not been caught. An investigation is undertaken to identify the perpetrator. The investigation will likely include the following: interviews of customers or employees who may have been present when the robbery occurred; inspection of the store and surrounding area to determine if the robber left any useful evidence such as fingerprints, DNA, a wallet, or other identifying information; viewing of security videotapes that may have been operating during the crime; and more. If the information discovered leads to prosecution of a crime or pursuit of a civil case, the investigator is typically an important witness at the trial.

Application to HP Facts: Sometimes the results of an investigation are inconclusive. Such was the circumstance with the Riddles' deaths.

The facts involving the dementors' attack were in dispute. Per the Ministry, the dementors could not have been where Harry said they were. Yet Harry and the Dursleys' neighbor, Mrs. Figg, both testified that the dementors were indeed in the Dursleys' neighborhood. This discrepancy in the facts is the type of circumstance that should trigger an investigation.

* * * * * * * * * * * * * *

Other Areas of Law Implicated by These Facts
Arrest
Due Process for Students at Suspension Hearings
Evidence
Innocent Until Proven Guilty

Other Areas of Law Implicated by These Facts (continued)

Justification

Murder

Restrictions on Minors

Right to an Attorney

Self-Defense and Defense of Others

CHAPTER 51

SEARCH AND SEIZURE

Raid and Ransack; Find and Filch

HP Facts: Lucias Malfoy, along with other Death Eaters, attempted to steal the Prophecy at the Ministry of Magic and was arrested. Members of the Ministry then raided the Malfoy house. They seized from it "everything that might have been dangerous." *(OOP-26,28; HBP-7)*

Muggle Law: The Federal Constitution contains a right against unreasonable search and seizure by an agent of the government such as a police officer. *Search and Seizure* refers to a probe of a person's property – such as a house, a suitcase or backpack – and confiscation of any evidence of a crime found during the search. The constitutional right is based on the principle that everyone is entitled to a reasonable amount of privacy from the police. Thus, law enforcement cannot on a whim, without any evidence, search our property. Instead, they must, in most circumstances, first obtain a *search warrant*. This is a written directive issued by a judge authorizing the police to search a person's possessions or house. Before a judge can issue a search warrant, the police must present evidence establishing *probable cause*. This means the police must have a threshold amount of evidence that would lead a person of reasonable caution to believe that something connected with a crime is located in the place the police want to search.

Exceptions to the Search Warrant Requirement. There are numerous exceptions to the general rule that police need a search warrant before they can legally search property. Among the exceptions are the following: consent to a search is given by the owner of the property; emergency circumstances exist and someone could be seriously injured or killed if a search is not undertaken; or the item seized is in plain view (as, for example, where you are stopped by police for a speeding charge and illegal drugs or other contraband are clearly visible on the passenger seat). An additional exception is a search incident to an arrest. With this exception, police are allowed to search the area in the immediate vicinity of someone who has just been arrested. This space is called the "grabbable area" because it is the area in which the person might reach out to grab a nearby weapon to use against the arresting officer, or to hide contraband.

Mall Security Officers. Another exception is a search conducted by a private person who is not acting as a governmental employee. For example, private security guards who protect malls are not police. They can legally inspect a shopper's backpack, pocketbook or shopping bag without the need for a search warrant. If, however, the guard is acting as an agent of the police, the right against unreasonable search and seizure applies. So, for example, if the security guard is assisting the police in an investigation at the mall and acts at the request or direction of the police, the guard needs either a search warrant or an applicable exception.

The Exclusionary Rule. This rule holds that if evidence is seized without a warrant and no exception to the warrant requirement applies, the evidence cannot be used at trial against the accused. Instead, the evidence is excluded (hence, the name – Exclusionary Rule). Without necessary evidence, the prosecutor will be unable to prove the case so charges against the accused are often dropped. This rule may seem ill-advised. However, the purpose is to encourage police to honor our constitutional right to be free from unreasonable searches of property we reasonably consider to be private. As a society, we would rather a guilty person go free than that police violate our privacy rights.

Application to HP Facts: The Ministry searched Lucias Malfoy's house. In the Muggle world, the Ministry would need either a search warrant or an applicable exception. At first glance, one exception may seem to apply – search incident to an arrest. However, the scope of this type of search is limited to the immediate vicinity around Lucias – the grabbable area. Lucias was arrested at the Ministry; the place searched was his house. Since the house is clearly way outside the grabbable area, the search would be illegal unless the Ministry had a warrant. If they searched without one, the Exclusionary Rule would apply: the evidence seized could not be used against Malfoy at a trial.

When the Exclusionary Rule applies, the only evidence that cannot be presented is the evidence obtained in violation of the right against unreasonable search and seizure. Other evidence available in the case and obtained legally is not tainted and remains usable at trial.

Consider the possibility that some of the items taken from Malfoy's house were illegal to possess. Assume that Malfoy was charged with the crime of illegal possession. If the Ministry did not have a warrant and the search was illegal, the items taken could not be used as evidence against him. If there were no other evidence to prove his guilt, the prosecution would be forced to withdraw the charge.

* * * * * * * * * * * * * *

Other Areas of Law Implicated by These Facts
Arrest
Evidence
Larceny
Trespass

CHAPTER 52

ARREST

Fudge Finds Feigned Facts

HP Facts: Following the attack on Muggle-borns by the Heir of Slytherin, Minister of Magic Cornelius Fudge arrived at Hagrid's hut with Professor Dumbledore. Fudge told Hagrid that Fudge was under pressure to do something about the attacks. Fudge was aware that Hagrid had been accused 50 years earlier of opening the Chamber of Secrets resulting in the death of Moaning Myrtle. Although we later learn that the accusation was unfounded, Fudge took Hagrid into custody and sent him to Azkaban Prison, all because of his "record." (*COS-14*)

Additional HP Facts: To save Harry from expulsion from Hogwarts, Professor Dumbledore confessed to Fudge and his Aurors that Dumbledore was responsible for the DA (Dumbledore's Army). The purpose of the organization, reported Dumbledore, was plotting against Fudge. In response, the Minister told Dumbledore that he would be "escorted to the Ministry where you will be formally charged and then sent to Azkaban to await trial." Dumbledore, however, surprised them all and escaped. (*OOP–27*)

Muggle Law: The constitutional right against unreasonable search and seizure that we studied in the prior chapter protects people not only from illegal searches but also from arrest by overzealous police. An arrest is the process of taking a suspect into custody by virtue of legal authority. Freedom is a precious right and is forfeited upon arrest. Therefore, the police cannot make an arrest without sufficient grounds. Needed is a threshold amount of evidence called *probable cause*. To satisfy the probable cause standard, the police must have

sufficient evidence to lead someone of reasonable caution to believe that the person arrested has committed a crime.

Arrest Warrant. In some circumstances, the police can arrest a suspect without a warrant and in other situations, a warrant is required. A warrant is an order from a judge directing a police officer to take custody of a specified individual and bring him to court to answer charges of criminal activity. Before a judge can issue an arrest warrant, the police must present evidence that convinces the judge that probable cause exists.

Illegal Arrest. If the police arrest a suspect without probable cause or a warrant, the arrest is illegal. Remedies include release of the defendant from custody and a civil lawsuit brought by the suspect against the police for the tort of false arrest seeking money to compensate for the unlawful confinement.

Application to HP Facts: Hagrid was taken into custody, and thereby arrested, by Fudge. The Minister had no justified basis to believe that Hagrid had done anything unlawful. Therefore, the arrest of Hagrid was illegal, and Hagrid should have been released. Hagrid could also sue the Ministry for money to compensate him for the unlawful restraint on his freedom.

Concerning Dumbledore, he confessed to plotting against Fudge by organizing the DA. The confession provides probable cause for the arrest.

Accio!

HP Facts: The head of the Department of Magical Law Enforcement Bob Ogden served a summons on Morfin Gaunt for violating Wizarding law by performing magic in front of a Muggle. Morfin had cast a spell that caused the Muggle to erupt in painful hives. The summons required Gaunt to attend a hearing at the Ministry of Magic. When Ogden approached Morfin's house to deliver the summons, Morfin drew a bloody knife and shot hexes from his wand, causing Ogden to run. He returned with reinforcements. Morfin and his father attempted to fight but were overpowered and taken to Azkaban. (*HBP-10*)

Muggle Law: As an alternative to arrest, the court or police can issue a summons which requires the recipient to appear in court on a given date and allows him to remain free in the interim. If the defendant does not appear at the designated time, the judge will likely issue an arrest warrant.

Application to HP Facts: Morfin's action indicated he would likely not attend court. His presence in court was assured by his subsequent arrest and removal to Azkaban.

* * * * * * * * * * * * * *

Other Areas of Law Implicated by These Facts
Assault and Battery – The Crime
Assault and Battery – The Torts
Evidence
Notice and Opportunity to Be Heard
Self-Incrimination/Confessions

CHAPTER 53

BOUNTY HUNTERS

Beware Snitches and Snatchers

HP Facts: During the search for Horcruxes, Ron temporarily left Harry and Hermione. When Ron rejoined the others, he said he would have returned sooner but he had been caught by Snatchers. Ron explained that Snatchers are gangs that earn gold by rounding up Muggle-borns and blood traitors and turning them into the Ministry of Magic for a reward. (*DH-19*) Snatchers use force to detain their captives, mistreat them, and steal possessions. Later, Harry, Hermione, and Ron were captured by Snatchers. Turns out, Harry had much to fear. Whereas the reward for a Mudblood was five Galleons, the reward for Harry, identified as Undesirable Number One, was 200,000 Galleons, a very desirable bounty. (*DH-23*)

Muggle Law: A bounty hunter is a person who captures fugitives for a money reward. A bounty hunter is sometimes called a bail enforcement agent or a fugitive recovery agent. To understand the role of the bounty hunter requires some knowledge of bail and bail bondsmen. Information about each follows.

Bail. After an arrest, a criminal defendant might be released from custody while the trial is pending or they may be detained in jail. The latter occurs when the judge believes the defendant might not return to court. An example of why a judge might think that is because the defendant previously failed to appear on a scheduled court date. Another reason would be that the defendant lives in another state and has no relatives, friends, or job in the vicinity of the court (no local ties). In such circumstances, the judge can impose *bail*. This refers to money exchanged for the release of a person who has been arrested. Bail is intended to motivate the defendant to return to court on

133

designated dates. If the defendant comes to court, the money is returned, usually at the end of the case. If the defendant fails to appear, the money is forfeited, meaning the defendant does not get it back.

Bail Bondsmen. The money for bail may be posted by a bail bondsman. This is a person who gives money or property to the court as bail. The bondsman typically collects from the defendant ten percent of the total amount of bail, which is then paid to the court. The bondsman usually will also require collateral from the defendant or his friends and relatives for the balance of the bail. The bondsman then guarantees to the court that the defendant will return when his case is next scheduled. The bondsman charges the defendant a fee for these services, which is typically ten percent of the original amount of the bail. If the defendant fails to show, the bondsman is required to pay to the court the full amount of the bail. To recoup his money, the bondsman is allowed by law to go looking for the defendant and bring him to court. Once the bondsman produces the defendant, the bondsman is entitled to reimbursement of the bail money. To assist in locating missing defendants, the law authorizes the bondsman to hire a bounty hunter – a person who captures fugitives for money.

Qualifications to be a bounty hunter vary from state to state. Typically, a bounty hunter is required to obtain a license issued by the state in which the hunter works; successfully complete a training program; work for one bail bondsman only; be at least 18 or 21 years old; and have no criminal record.

Application to HP Facts: The Snatchers were in the business of capturing people wanted by the Ministry. They appeared to be mercenary thugs and may have had a criminal record. We are not told whether they had a license. Thus, they would likely fail to qualify as bounty hunters for several reasons. Also, bounty hunters cannot capture people just because someone is undesirable or lacks a certain Blood Status.

134

* * * * * * * * * * * * *

Other Areas of Law Implicated by These Facts
Assault and Battery – The Crime
Assault and Battery – The Torts
False Imprisonment
Kidnapping
Legal Tender
Robbery

CHAPTER 54

INFORMANTS AND IMMUNITY

Telltale Characters

HP Facts: The first gathering of Hogwarts students who would become the DA (Dumbledore's Army) took place at the Hogs Head Tavern in the Village of Hogsmead. Sitting at the bar was an unidentifiable person who was wrapped in dirty bandages and kept his head hidden. Later, when Professor Umbridge confronted Harry about the DA, she told him that Willy Widdershins had provided information about the organization. Turns out Widdershins was the one covered in bandages at the Hog's Head and overheard the discussions at the bar. He had been earlier caught jinxing Muggle toilets so they would regurgitate. When Harry told Professor McGonagall about Widdershins disclosure to Umbridge, McGonagall commented that she now understood why Widdershins was never prosecuted for rigging the regurgitating toilets. (*OOP-16, 27*)

Additional HP Facts: The DA was an outlawed club at Hogwarts. Cho Chang's friend Marietta Edgecomb, who had attended the first meeting, reported to Umbridge about the organization. Umbridge, in the presence of Professor Dumbledore, Minister of Magic Cornelius Fudge, and Harry, interrogated Marietta for confirmation of the DA's existence and purpose. However, Hermione had put a jinx on everyone who participated in the DA causing pustules (pimple-like growths) to appear on their face spelling out the word "sneak" for anyone who disclosed information about the organization. Horrified by her pocked face, Marietta refused to speak further. (*OOP-27*)

Additional HP Facts: On one of Harry's trips into Dumbledore's Pensieve, Harry encountered Igor Karkaroff, a

136

convicted Death Eater serving time at Azkaban Prison. In the memory, the Ministry of Magic was trying to round up the last of the Dark Lord's supporters. Karkaroff had struck a deal with the Ministry that if Karkaroff provided names of Voldemort's supporters not previously known to the Ministry, he would be released from Azkaban. Karkaroff was then brought before the Ministry to provide names of other Death Eaters. (*GOF-30*)

Muggle Law: When police investigate a crime they rely in part on witnesses to the criminal acts. Sometimes, witnesses refuse to come forward. Sometimes, there are no witnesses. To obtain needed information, an acceptable police practice is to consult participants in the crime or other criminals who happen to have knowledge about the case, both of whom are called informants. Without some kind of incentive, potential informants are not likely to disclose what they know. To make it worthwhile, police may offer immunity (freedom from prosecution) or leniency (such as a shortened jail sentence) in exchange for their information.

As you might anticipate, informants are regarded as traitors by their criminal partners. If the partner learns of the informant's cooperation with the police, the informant is at risk for retaliation. To avoid harm, police sometimes provide protection to informants, which can include segregation in jail or, if they are not imprisoned, living arrangements in a new city and a new identity. The latter is generally known as the Witness Protection Program. As part of the Program, the witness receives a new name as well as new identification documents such as a driver's license.

Application to HP Facts: McGonagall surmised that Widdershins had negotiated a deal to become an informant. In return for telling Umbridge what he learned about the DA at the tavern, Widdershins was given immunity from prosecution for the regurgitating toilets. In Muggle law, this deal would be an enforceable contract. Apparently, it worked in the

Wizarding world as well since Willy was not charged with disrupting the toilets.

Concerning Marietta Edgecomb, while the book does not specifically identify what benefit she expected from telling Umbridge about the DA, we can assume she would have been excused from punishment for having attended a DA meeting.

Karkaroff, as an informant, made a contract with the Ministry. To satisfy his part of the arrangement, he needed to provide names of Death Eaters who had not previously been identified. The first two names he gave were already known to the Ministry and so would not have won his release. He was, however, able to provide one name of value, Augustus Roockwood, and the Ministry agreed to assess whether the name was worth Karkaroff's release. Given that Karkaroff subsequently became the headmaster of Durmstrang, we can conclude the Ministry was satisfied and he was released.

* * * * * * * * * * * * * *

Other Areas of Law Implicated by These Facts
Criminal Mischief/Vandalism
Eavesdropping and Wiretapping
Freedom of Contract
Freedom of Assembly

CHAPTER 55

NOTICE AND OPPORTUNITY TO BE HEARD

Hear Me Out

HP Facts: Harry used magic to defend himself and Dudley against an attack by the dementors. He received notice via owl from the Ministry of Magic that a hearing would be held to determine whether he should be expelled from Hogwarts for underage use of magic. The notice advised him of the time and place of the hearing. At the last minute, and unbeknownst to Harry, the time of the hearing was moved up by several hours. Relying on the time stated in the notice he received, Harry almost missed the proceeding. *(OOP-2,8)*

Additional HP Facts: Sirius Black had been accused of causing the deaths of 12 Muggles and Peter Pettigrew. Based upon a directive from Barty Crouch, Sr., Sirius was sent to Azkaban Prison without a trial. *(GOF-27)*

Muggle Law: Our Federal Constitution guarantees a group of rights embodied in the term d*ue process*. When the government charges someone with a crime, the right to due process entitles the defendant to a trial. Likewise, if the government seeks to revoke a privilege, such as cancelling a driver's license or expelling a student from school, the person targeted is entitled to a hearing. At the trial or hearing, the government must prove that the defendant did something wrong. Likewise, the person accused has the right to present witnesses to rebut the government's evidence. This is called the right to be heard and is an integral part of due process. Also included is the right to advance notice of the time and location of the trial or hearing. The purpose of the notice is in part to give the defendant time to prepare a defense and locate witnesses. Notice also serves to inform the defendant when and where to appear to present his defense.

Application to HP Facts: The last minute change in the time of Harry's hearing, making it earlier than stated on the written notice, might have caused Harry to miss the proceeding. Had that happened, he would have lost the opportunity to present his defense. In that circumstance, if the decision from the Wizengamot had been unfavorable, Harry would have been entitled to a new hearing based on the due process violation.

Black's prolonged imprisonment without a trial was a serious violation of his right to be heard.

* * * * * * * * * * * * *

Other Areas of Law Implicated by These Facts

Due Process for Students at Suspension Hearings
Justification
Restrictions on Minors
Self-Defense and Defense of Others

CHAPTER 56

RIGHT TO AN UNBIASED JUDGE

Free From Taint

HP Facts: Harry used magic to repel the dementor attack on him and his cousin Dudley in Little Whinging. For this, Harry was accused of violating the Decree for the Reasonable Restriction of Underage Sorcery and the International Confederation of Wizards' Statute of Secrecy. Harry was tried before the full Wizengamot, a court of 50 judges. The Minister of Magic, Cornelius Fudge, served as the presiding judge and interrogator. It was clear from Fudge's conduct that he believed Harry was guilty before the trial even started. He would not permit Harry the opportunity to tell his story fully and all but accused Harry of lying. Fudge tried to prevent Professor Dumbledore from presenting evidence in Harry's defense, saying there was not time and he wanted "this dealt with quickly." (*OOP-1,8*)

Additional HP Facts: Following the take-over of the Ministry of Magic by Voldemort, the Muggle-born Registration Commission was formed. This required all Muggle-borns (witches or wizards with non-magical parents) to register with the Ministry and to present themselves before the Commission to be interviewed. The stated purpose of the Commission was to ensure that witches or wizards did not obtain their magical powers by theft. Unless the Muggle-borns could prove magical ancestry, they could be sent to Azkaban Prison on suspicion of theft. The Head of the Commission was none other than Dolores Umbridge. At the hearing regarding Elizabeth Cattermole, Umbridge's statement and the way she treated Mrs. Cattermole made it clear that Umbridge had made up her mind before beginning the proceeding. After Harry and Hermione helped Mrs. Cattermole escape from the Ministry,

Hermione advised the woman to get out of the country as she "won't get anything like a fair hearing here." (*DH–11,13*)

Muggle Law: The constitutional right to due process requires fairness in court proceedings including the right to an unbiased judge. If a judge in a criminal case has decided the defendant is guilty before the trial or hearing even begins, the right of a defendant to present evidence and defend himself becomes moot. When judges are unable to be impartial in a case, they should *recuse* themselves. This means they should decline to hear the case and instead refer it to another judge.

Application to HP Facts: Harry was accused of violating the law and risked being expelled from Hogwarts. He was entitled to a trial or hearing at which the school must prove his alleged infraction, and he has an opportunity to present evidence, cross-examine opposing witnesses, and receive a ruling from the judge based on the evidence presented. Fudge had predetermined Harry's guilt and attempted to influence the other members of the Wizengamot. The Minister's premature conclusion impacted his actions as presiding judge and interrogator, to the disadvantage of Harry. Fudge's participation at the hearing violated Harry's right to an unbiased judge. The Minister should have recused himself from the case.

Umbridge's apparent advanced determination that Mrs. Cattermole obtained her magical powers illegally violated Mrs. Cattermole's right to an unbiased judge.

* * * * * * * * * * * * * *

Other Areas of Law Implicated by These Facts
Evidence
Equal Protection
Innocent Until Proven Guilty
Justification

Other Areas of Law Implicated by These Facts (continued)

Notice and Opportunity to Be Heard
Restrictions on Minors
Right to an Attorney
Self-Defense and Defense of Others

CHAPTER 57

RIGHT TO AN ATTORNEY

An Advocate to Advocate

HP Facts: Harry received a letter informing him that he was required to attend a disciplinary hearing that was to be held in a courtroom at the Ministry of Magic. Harry was accused of violating the Decree of the Reasonable Restriction of Underage Sorcery and also the International Confederation of Wizards Statute of Secrecy. The charges related to Harry's having conjured a Patronus outside of Hogwarts and in the presence of a Muggle (cousin Dudley). Harry was not told that he had a right to counsel or other representation at the hearing, nor was a lawyer or other advocate provided. Fortunately, Professor Dumbledore appeared saying he was a "witness" for Harry. His actions at the hearing, however, were more akin to that of a defense lawyer. Dumbledore called Mrs. Figg as a witness for Harry, and he presented arguments to the Wizengamot supporting Harry's position. (*OOP–2,8*)

Muggle Law: Court proceedings are run according to rigorous rules that can impact the outcome of a case. Lawyers learn these rules in law school. They are generally unknown by non-lawyers. Defendants are thus at a significant disadvantage if they are not represented by an attorney. Much is at stake including a person's freedom (possible prison time) or even life (possible death sentence). For fairness, the right to due process includes the right of defendants in criminal cases to have a competent attorney. If they cannot afford one, the government will provide a lawyer for them, often called a public defender. The financial threshold that entitles a criminal defendant to a free attorney is determined by government guidelines.

Application to HP Facts: If Harry were charged with a crime, he would have been entitled to a lawyer at his hearing. However, the charge did not appear to subject him to restrictions on his freedom such as jail time. Instead, the penalty he faced was expulsion from school. The right to an attorney does not apply to a school suspension hearing. Nonetheless, some schools permit students to bring an advocate to such a hearing. The facts of Harry's hearing are instructive on the importance to the person accused of having a knowledgeable advocate to assist in any legal or quasi-legal proceeding.

* * * * * * * * * * * * *

Other Areas of Law Implicated by These Facts

Due Process for Students at Suspension Hearings
Evidence
Justification
Notice and Opportunity to be Heard
Right to an Unbiased Judge
Self-Defense and Defense of Others

CHAPTER 58

EVIDENCE

An Alley, Two Cats, and a Mark

HP Facts: Two dementors attacked Harry and Dudley in an alleyway near Privet Drive. Harry used magic to repel them, resulting in his school suspension hearing. The Dursleys' neighbor, Mrs. Figg, happened to see the dementor attack while walking home from the corner shop where she had bought cat food. At the hearing, Minister of Magic Fudge openly doubted Harry's testimony contending instead that dementors could not have been anywhere near the Dursleys' home. Mrs. Figg then testified on Harry's behalf about the dementor attack. (*OOP-1,8*)

Additional HP Facts: Throughout *Prisoner of Azkaban*, Ron and Hermione frequently bickered because Hermione's cat Crookshanks had designs on Ron's rat Scabbers. One day Ron found a bloodstain on his bed sheet and cat hairs nearby. Ron, upset, confronted Hermione, accusing Crookshanks of killing Scabbers.
(*POA-12*)

Additional HP Facts: After Ireland won the Quidditch World Cup, Death Eaters marched through the camp causing fear and destruction. Suddenly, the Dark Mark appeared in the sky. Ministry of Magic officials searched for the person who conjured it. Barty Crouch, Sr.'s house elf Winky was found in the area and was holding Harry's wand. The Ministry determined that the Dark Mark was conjured from that wand. Winky was accused of conjuring the Dark Mark. (*GOF-9*)

Additional HP Facts: Harry, Ron, and Hermione were walking down a corridor at Hogwarts when they came across Mr. Filch's cat, Mrs. Norris. She had been petrified and was hanging by her tail from a torch bracket. Nearby, writing on the wall in blood announced that the Heir of Slytherin had returned, and the Chamber of Secrets had been opened. Harry was standing by Mrs. Norris when others, including Filtch, arrived. Filtch believed Harry was the culprit and demanded punishment. (*COS-8, 9*)

Muggle Law: Evidence is critical to a lawsuit. By definition, evidence is information (testimony and documents) as well as other tangible (sometimes called physical) items that tend to prove facts. Examples include blood, hair, DNA, weapons, and illegal drugs. All evidence is either direct or circumstantial.

Direct Evidence. Direct evidence includes both testimony from a witness who saw or heard something relevant to the commission of a crime, plus relevant documents and physical evidence. An example of direct evidence is Mrs. Figg's testimony that she observed the dementors.

Circumstantial Evidence. Circumstantial evidence is sometimes referred to as "connecting the dots." It implies that something occurred but does not directly prove the occurrence. For example, two students hand in an assignment to their teacher. The content on both students' papers is identical, word-for-word. If someone had seen one student copy the other's homework, we would have direct evidence of cheating. Instead, the only evidence is that the two papers are exactly the same. The odds of that happening without one copying from the other are small. The similarity in the work is circumstantial evidence of cheating.

Direct evidence is not necessary to win a civil lawsuit or convict a criminal defendant. Circumstantial evidence can be sufficient. Whenever circumstantial evidence is used, the jury must decide whether or not to draw the inference that the alleged fact occurred. Sometimes, the inferred fact is exactly

147

what happened. Other times, the inferred fact was not what transpired, although the circumstantial evidence made it seem very likely.

Application to HP Facts. All three referenced HP Facts illustrate circumstantial evidence. The fact finder (Ron/the Ministry officials/Hogwarts staff) must make a decision whether or not to draw the inference.

In all three examples, the circumstantial evidence proves unreliable. We learn that, despite the apparent evidence connecting Crookshanks to Scabbers' supposed death, Scabbers did not die, and Crookshanks did not harm him. Similarly, although at first glance, Winky looks guilty of using Harry's wand to create the Dark Mark, she did not do it. And Harry had nothing to do with poor Mrs. Norris' petrified condition. These circumstances point out the limitations of circumstantial evidence. Nonetheless, this type of proof is critical in cases where direct evidence is not available.

* * * * * * * * * * * * * *

Other Areas of Law Implicated by These Facts
Due Process for Students and Suspension Hearing
Investigations
Innocent Until Proven Guilty
Notice and Opportunity to Be Heard
Right to an Attorney
Right to an Unbiased Judge
Self-Defense and Defense of Others

CHAPTER 59

INNOCENT UNTIL PROVEN GUILTY

Jumping to Conclusions

HP Facts: Harry, Ron, and Hermione encountered Mr. Filch's cat, Mrs. Norris, petrified in a corridor at Hogwarts. Writing on the wall nearby in blood said that the Heir of Slytherin had returned and that the Chamber of Secrets had been opened. Initially, because Harry was standing by Mrs. Norris when others arrived, Filch accused Harry of killing the cat and was demanding punishment. Professors Snape and McGonagall were among those who came to the scene. Harry denied involvement, but Snape was unconvinced and suggested that Harry should not be allowed to play on the Gryffindor Quidditch team "until he is ready to be honest." McGonagall pointed out that there was no evidence that Harry was involved. She said to Snape, "Innocent until proven guilty, Severus." (*COS-9*)

Additional HP Facts: Following the take-over of the Ministry of Magic by Voldemort, the Muggle-born Registration Commission was formed. This required all Muggle-borns (witches or wizards with non-magical parents) to register with the Ministry and to present themselves before the Commission to be interviewed. The stated purpose of the Commission was to ensure that witches or wizards did not obtain their magical powers by theft. Unless the Muggle-born witches or wizards could prove magical ancestry, they could be sent to Azkaban Prison on suspicion of theft. Thus, the Commission considered them guilty until proven innocent. (*DH–11*)

Muggle Law: A person accused of a crime has the right to a presumption of innocence. This means the defendant is considered by law to be innocent until proven guilty. He

149

cannot be treated as guilty unless and until the prosecution presents evidence at a trial sufficient to convince a jury or a judge that the defendant is guilty. To overcome the presumption, the prosecutor must present evidence to prove the defendant's guilt *beyond a reasonable doubt*. This means for a jury or judge to find a defendant guilty, they must have no reasonable doubt of the defendant's guilt at the end of the trial. A reasonable doubt is a doubt that a reasonable person might entertain after a careful review of all the evidence in a case. It is more than a whim, guess, or surmise and, instead, must have some basis in fact. If a reasonable doubt exists after all the evidence has been presented, the presumption of innocence remains, and the defendant must be found not guilty.

Application to HP Facts: Harry was in the wrong place at the wrong time. Circumstances made it appear that he was responsible for the feline foul play. Professor Snape's suggestion of barring Harry from the Quidditch team was premature. As Professor McGonagall cautioned Snape, Harry should not be disciplined unless and until his guilt was established. Prior to such time, he is entitled to the presumption of innocence, rendering punishment inappropriate.

Similarly, wizards and witches appearing before the Muggle Registration Commission would be entitled to a presumption of innocence. Rather than having to prove their magical ancestry, the Commission should have to prove that the witch or wizard obtained their magical powers by theft.

＊＊＊＊＊＊＊＊＊＊＊＊＊＊

Other Areas of Law Implicated by These Facts
Equal Protection
Evidence

CHAPTER 60

SELF-INCRIMINATION/CONFESSIONS

Silence is Golden

HP Facts: Harry and Dumbledore viewed various memories in the Pensieve to piece together parts of Voldemort's past. After seeing memories related to Morfin Gaunt and Hokey the house elf, Dumbledore informs Harry what happened after each memory. Dumbledore tells Harry that Morfin confessed to killing Tom Riddle's father and grandparents, and that as a result of such confession, Morfin was convicted of these murders, and Morfin was sent to Azkaban where he later died. Dumbledore also informs Harry that Hokey was convicted of poisoning her mistress Hepzibah after Hokey confessed to putting a little-known poison in her mistress's drink. Ironically, despite both Morfin's and Hokey's confessions, neither was the culprit who committed the killings. Rather, their memories had been modified by the real killer, Tom Riddle. Riddle's motivation in framing Morfin and Hokey was to steal Morfin's ring and Hepzibah's cup to use them as Horcruxes. *(HBP-17,20)*

Muggle Law: *Miranda Warnings.* A criminal defendant has a constitutional right not to incriminate himself (right against self-incrimination). This means he is not required to answer any questions the police might ask, and he is not required to provide any explanation or information relating to the charge. If the police wish to question the accused while he is in custody (under police control and not free to leave), the officer must first read him his "Miranda Warnings" (also called Miranda Rights). This means the officer must inform the defendant of the following:

- You have the right to remain silent.

- Anything you say can and will be used against you in a court of law.
- You have the right to consult an attorney.
- If you cannot afford an attorney, one will be hired for you.
- Do you understand what I have just said?
- Do you agree to waive your rights and answer my questions?

If the defendant says no or asks for an attorney, the police must stop the questioning. If an officer continues to question the defendant, any answers he might give will be suppressed, meaning they will not be admissible in court. If the police question the defendant while he is in custody without reading the Miranda Warnings, the statements will likely be suppressed.

Sometimes a suspect spontaneously volunteers information without being questioned by the police. There is no duty to read the rights prior to such statements. Indeed, since this type of statement occurs without warning, the officers would not be able to predict when the warnings should be read. A spontaneous, voluntary statement is admissible as evidence at trial notwithstanding the fact that Miranda Warnings were not read.

Corroboration Required for Conviction. In most states, a defendant cannot be convicted based on his confession alone. Some additional evidence is required to establish that the crime was, in fact, committed. This additional information is called corroboration. The purpose of this rule is to ensure that a person is not convicted of a crime that never occurred. You may be wondering why anyone would admit to a crime he did not commit. There are numerous reasons. They include mental health issues; intoxication; desire to protect the wrongdoer; and aggressive police tactics, such as threats of harm or exaggerated predictions of the outcome if the defendant fails to confess. Sadly, numerous defendants have been wrongfully convicted and imprisoned based on a police-coerced confession. Recent developments involving DNA evidence have assisted in securing these defendants exoneration and release from jail.

Application to HP Facts: The reader is not told that Miranda Warnings were read to either Morfin or Hokey. If their confessions were made during police questioning while they were in custody, and if the rights were not read, their statements would be suppressed. On the other hand, if the statements were volunteered by Morfin and Hokey without being prompted by police, the statements would be admissible even though Miranda Warnings were not read.

Concerning the corroboration requirement, the bodies of Riddle's father and grandparents provided the necessary evidence that a crime was committed independent of Morfin's confession. The body of Hepzibah provided the needed corroboration for Hokey's confession. Unfortunately for both Morfin and Hokey, no requirement exists for corroboration of the perpetrator's identity.

* * * * * * * * * * * * *

Other Areas of Law Implicated by These Facts
Larceny
Murder
Right to an Attorney
Sentencing

CHAPTER 61

LIE DETECTORS

The Truth, the Whole Truth, and Nothing But the Truth

HP Facts: Professor Snape, during one of his tirades in class, accused Harry of breaking into his office and stealing potion ingredients including boomslang skin (needed for Polyjuice Potion) and Gillyweed. In response to Harry's denial, Snape displayed a bottle of Veritaserum, a truth potion, and threatened to spill some into Harry's evening pumpkin juice. (*GOF-27*)

Additional HP Facts: When the fake Mad Eye Moody is exposed to be Barty Crouch, Jr., Dumbledore directs Snape to give the imposter Veritaserum to learn the reason why he impersonated Mad Eye Moody. Much to the horror of Winky the house elf, Crouch, Jr. tells all, proving the effectiveness of the potion. (*GOF-35)*

Muggle Law: An instrument exists called a lie detector (its official name is a polygraph) that has some, but limited, use in the courts. Despite its name, it is not able to reliably detect if a person is lying. Rather, it can identify when the person exhibits fluctuations in certain physical characteristics that are sometimes – but not always – associated with deceptive behavior such as lying. The instrument does so by monitoring certain vital signs – heart rate, blood pressure, respiratory rate, and sweatiness in fingers. Fluctuations can be caused by a variety of factors; lying is only one possibility. Therein lies the unreliability of the lie detector's results. Due to the possibility of inaccurate readings, defendants have the right to refuse to submit to a lie detector test. Further, the results are barred by use at trial unless both parties agree to allow them in, with one exception. New Mexico allows admission of the results without the need for the agreement of the parties.

Application to HP Facts: In the Muggle world Snape would not be able to use the Veritaserum without Harry and Crouch's okay.

* * * * * * * * * * * * *

Other Areas of Law Implicated by These Facts
Identity Theft
Larceny
Self-Incrimination/Confessions

CHAPTER 62

APPEALS

Buckbeak's Second Chance

HP Facts: Most unfortunately, during Hagrid's first class as Professor of the Care of Magical Creatures, Buckbeak the hippogriff slashed Draco Malfoy with a talon, causing Draco injury. In typical Malfoy form, he exaggerated the damage to make Hagrid look bad. Draco's father Lucias filed a complaint with the Committee for the Disposal of Dangerous Creatures. Hagrid received a notice informing him of a hearing to address the matter. After the hearing, Hagrid learned that the Committee ruled against Buckbeak and sentenced the hippogriff to be executed. Thereafter, Hagrid notified Harry that a date for Buckbeak's appeal had been set. (*POA-6,15*)

Muggle Law: The losing party in a lawsuit or criminal prosecution can request that a higher court review the proceedings of the previous court. This process is called an *appeal*. In most cases, the parties can appeal several times. In each round, a new judge or panel of judges assesses the decision of the earlier court. If a significant error is found by judges during an appeal, the prior decision may be overturned and a new trial scheduled.

Application to HP Facts: In the Muggle world, Hagrid would have the right to appeal the Committee's decision to end Buckbeak's life.

* * * * * * * * * * * * * *

Other Areas of Law Implicated by These Facts
Due Process for Animals
In Loco Parentis
Right to an Unbiased Judge

156

CHAPTER 63

SENTENCING

The Price You Pay

HP Facts: Morfin Gaunt was accused of violating Wizarding law by performing magic in the presence of Muggles. Specifically, Gaunt was charged with performing a jinx on Riddle's Muggle father, causing him to break out in painful hives. Bob Ogden, head of the Magical Law Enforcement Squad, attempted to serve a summons on Morfin at his cabin. "With a roar of rage," Morfin ran towards Ogden waving a bloody knife and shooting hexes from his wand, causing Ogden to run. He apparated to the Ministry of Magic and returned to Morfin's hut fifteen minutes later with reinforcements, apparently to arrest Morfin. He and his father Marvolo Gaunt fought the Ministry representatives in an attempt to discourage them from prosecuting the matter. The Gaunts were overpowered and taken before the Wizengamot. Both Gaunts were convicted, apparently of assault of Ogden and his colleagues and likely also of resisting arrest. Morfin was probably also convicted of assault for the attack on the Muggle. Morfin, who had a history of Muggle attacks, was sentenced to three years in Azkaban Prison. Marvolo, who injured several Ministry employees in the wrangle over the arrest but apparently had no previous record, was sentenced to six months in Azkaban. (*HBP–10*)

Muggle Law: A defendant found guilty of a crime is sentenced by a judge. The sentence can include jail time, a fine, *probation* (the defendant is released into the community under the supervision of a probation officer in lieu of jail), community service, home confinement, treatment (for example, alcohol or drug counseling or an anger management program), or an educational program (such as defensive driving). The sentence for each case is tailored to the

157

circumstances, needs, and record of the defendant. Thus, it is possible that two people committing similar crimes will be sentenced differently.

To determine the appropriate sentence, the judge considers the following four factors: seriousness of the crime, its impact on the victim and the community, defendant's circumstances (such as age, health, job status), and defendant's criminal record.

Application of HP Facts: Morfin was sentenced to three years in jail and Marvolo only six months. Yet they both engaged in the same criminal conduct against the Ministry representatives. The difference in the sentences is likely due to the following aggravating facts applicable to Morfin: he had a prior record of attacking Muggles; he likely was convicted of the attack against Riddle's father; and he not only attacked Ogden's reinforcements, but he also attacked Ogden on the initial visit to the Gaunts' residence.

* * * * * * * * * * * * *

Other Areas of Law Implicated by These Facts
Arrest
Assault and Battery – The Crime
Assault and Battery – The Torts

CHAPTER 64

DEATH PENALTY

A Foul Kiss

HP Facts: Sirius Black was accused of murdering one wizard and 12 Muggles. He was sent to Azkaban Prison for life for these crimes. For most convicts, this is viewed as a death sentence or worse. Being around the dementors for years on end will usually drive a prisoner mad, eventually leading to death. In some instances, the Ministry of Magic authorizes the dementors to perform the "Dementor's Kiss." They clamp their jaws on the mouth of the victim and suck out his soul. This is thought to be worse than death because it leaves the person as an empty shell, without a sense of self or memory and with no chance of recovery. Following Sirius' escape from Azkaban, the Ministry authorized the dementors to perform the Kiss on him immediately upon his capture. Had Harry and Hermione not rescued Sirius, the Kiss would have been performed. (*POA-12*)

Muggle Law: The most serious penalties for criminal conduct apply to defendants who are convicted of the most serious crimes. Those penalties include life in prison, life in prison without parole, and the death penalty.

Life Sentence. This sentence sounds like the defendant will spend the balance of his life in jail. However, the name is misleading. With a life sentence, the defendant must serve a minimum amount of time in prison which is usually quite lengthy (for example, 20 years or longer). Once that minimum term is completed, the defendant becomes eligible for *parole.* Parole means the defendant is released conditionally from jail after serving a portion of his sentence. To remain out of prison, he must comply with many terms and conditions of parole, including refraining from criminal activity, meeting regularly with a parole officer, and seeking a job or participating in job training. The parole officer's job is to assist and supervise the defendant. Eligibility for parole does not mean the prisoner will in fact be paroled. Rather, parole must be approved by a Parole Board, whose members are typically appointed by the governor.

Life in Prison without Parole. A sentence that is gaining in popularity as an alternative to the death penalty is life in jail without parole. As the name suggests, with this sentence, the defendant spends the remainder of his life in jail without the possibility of release on parole.

Death Penalty. The death penalty, also called capital punishment, is the execution (killing) of a convicted criminal by the government as punishment for the conviction of a crime referred to as *capital crimes* or *capital offenses*. Approximately two-thirds of the states have death penalty statutes. The crimes that are punishable by the death penalty are, not surprisingly, the most heinous. They include primarily intentional murder committed with an aggravating factor. Examples of such factors are: a police officer was the victim; more than one person was killed; the victim was tortured; the killer was already in jail for life; or the death occurred during a terrorist act. Additionally, in a few jurisdictions, the following crimes subject the perpetrator to the possibility of execution: hijacking an airplane; aggravated sexual assault; aggravated kidnapping; perjury causing execution; and treason.

The death penalty has long generated controversy. Supporters believe it deters crimes and is a justified consequence for taking another person's life. Supporters also point out that the death penalty ensures the defendant will not be a repeat offender victimizing additional people. Opponents argue that capital punishment violates the criminal's right to life; does not deter criminals any more than life imprisonment does; discriminates against minorities and the poor (indeed, at least one state has imposed a moratorium on the death penalty pending further study of racial and economic disparities); and can result in the execution of a person who was wrongly convicted.[2]

Application to HP Facts: Had Black, in fact, murdered 13 people, he would have been eligible for the death penalty in those states that impose it. The applicable aggravating factor to his crime is that he allegedly killed more than one person. However, had he been accorded his due process rights, including an opportunity to defend himself at a trial, he would have been acquitted had the truth come out.

* * * * * * * * * * * * *

Other Areas of Law Implicated by These Facts
Innocent Until Proven Guilty
Notice and Opportunity to be Heard
Sentencing

---

[2] Tragically, innocent people are sometimes found guilty. Fortunately, the advent of DNA evidence in the last ten years significantly reduces the possibility of this occurring. See *www.innocenceproject.org*.

VIII.

NON-CRIMINAL WRONGS (TORTS)

CHAPTER 65

NEGLIGENCE

Lockhart Needs Boning-Up on His Spells

HP Facts: During a Quidditch match, Harry was struck by a rogue Bludger that broke his arm. The inept Professor Lockhart proclaimed that he would fix it. Despite Harry's protests (based on doubts about Lockhart's true abilities), Lockhart pointed his wand at Harry and cast a spell. Almost immediately a "strange and unpleasant" feeling spread from Harry's shoulder to his fingertips He felt his arm deflate as though air was escaping from a balloon. Turns out, not only did Lockhart's spell not cure Harry's arm, it caused the bones to disappear! Harry was rushed to the hospital wing at Hogwarts where, fortunately, Madam Pomfrey was able to restore the bones with the help of Skele-Gro. The process was quite painful so Harry spent a very uncomfortable night. (*COS-10*)

Muggle Law: At all times, people are required by law to act carefully to avoid harm to others. Failure to exercise a reasonable degree of caution creates a risk of injury and constitutes *negligence*. A person who acts negligently is liable to anyone injured by his actions. When a person acts negligently in the performance of professional services – such as a doctor, dentist, accountant, or lawyer – the relevant term is *malpractice*. The careless professional may be liable for any resulting injuries.

Examples of negligence include failing to inspect the floor of a restaurant dining room before allowing diners to enter for lunch. If a customer slips on a food item, such as a piece of macaroni that had been lying on the ground for awhile, the restaurant may be liable for negligence. If a motorist fails to stop at a red light and injures a pedestrian crossing the street, that too is negligence. If a dentist extracts the wrong tooth by mistake, that constitutes malpractice. In all three examples, the negligent party may be liable to pay for injuries caused from his carelessness.

163

To be successful in a lawsuit based on negligence, the plaintiff must prove not only carelessness, but two additional facts as well: the plaintiff suffered an injury, and the injury was caused by the negligence.

Application to HP Facts: Lockhart knew his purported skills were greatly exaggerated. He had no basis for thinking he could re-grow Harry's bones. Yet, he tried a spell to mend the bones, which, predictably, did not work and caused Harry's condition to worsen. Lockhart would thus be liable to Harry for his negligent attempt to cure Harry's arm.

* * * * * * * * * * * * *

Other Areas of Law Implicated by These Facts
Assumption of Risk
Informed Consent
In Loco Parentis

CHAPTER 66

DEFAMATION

Quick-Quote Quills Cause Quivering

HP Facts: Rita Skeeter used a Quick-Quotes Quill to write an article for the *Daily Prophet* about Harry's competing in the Triwizard Tournament. However, the quill was not writing the answers to questions posed to Harry, but rather whatever Rita was thinking. For example, while Harry was dry-eyed talking about his parents, the quill wrote, "Tears fill those startlingly green eyes as our conversation turns to the parents he can barely remember." After reading the article, some Slytherins made snide remarks to Harry such as, "Want a hanky, Potter, in case you start crying in Transfiguration"? (*GOF-18, 19*)

Muggle Law: *Defamation* is a tort that consists of publicizing untruthful, demeaning statements about a person. "Publicize" means telling the false information to someone else, not just to the person about whom the lie was told. If I falsely accuse you of stealing, and no one else is in hearing range, this is not defamation. However, if one of your friends is present, my comment has been "publicized."

The fabrication must injure the person's reputation. For example, if you were told that one of your favorite teachers sold illegal drugs, your view of that instructor would change. Rather than the respect you used to have for him, you would likely now view him less favorably. If, in fact, the teacher did not commit the crime, he would have grounds to sue for defamation.

Defamation is also known by two other names – *slander* and *libel.* Slander refers to oral defamation (spoken); libel refers to written defamation (such as in newspapers or on the Internet).

Application to HP Facts: Rita Skeeter reported that Harry cries when he thinks about his parents but this was not true. Harry suffered damages by having to endure the teasing of Draco and his cohorts. Nonetheless, this statement is not defamation because it does not demean Harry. Although some students made fun of him, there is no shame in caring enough about people we love that thoughts of their death bring us to tears. Instead, the ability to love deeply is generally considered an enviable trait.

Hermione, the "Muggle-Born"

HP Facts: Rita wrote several times about Hermione. In one article, she is described as a "Muggle-born girl." *(GOF-19)*

Muggle Law: By definition, defamation requires an untruthful statement. Truth is a complete defense. Truthful statements, even though they may be insulting, hurtful, or damaging, are not illegal.

Application to HP Facts: In the Wizarding world, the term "Muggle-born" is an insult. However, Hermione's parents are in fact Muggles. Because truth is a complete defense, these statements are not defamation.

The Opinion Exception: The Ugly and The Dingbat

HP Facts: Pansy Parkinson is quoted as saying that Hermione "is really ugly but she'd be well up to making a Love Potion." *(GOF-27)* In an article about the International Confederation of Wizards' Conference, Skeeter referred to Professor Dumbledore as an "obsolete dingbat." *(GOF-18)*

Muggle Law: *Exception for Opinion.* Everyone is entitled to an opinion, even one that is unflattering to someone else. For example, you may not like a comedian's brand of comedy, and you are free to say so; such statements do not ordinarily constitute defamation.

Application to HP Facts: The quote by Pansy Parkinson referring to Hermione as "really ugly" is Pansy's opinion and, therefore, is not defamation. Similarly, Rita's comment that Professor Dumbledore was an "obsolete dingbat" constitutes an opinion and so is not libel.

Hagrid/Maim; Rita/Lame

HP Facts: Rita published a very unfavorable article in the *Daily Prophet* about Hagrid. It stated, "Hagrid has maimed several pupils during a series of lessons that many admit to being very frightening." That sentence was followed by a quote from Draco Malfoy, "I was attacked by a hippogriff, and my friend Vincent Crabbe got a bad bite off a flobberworm." *(GOF-24)*

Muggle Law: When determining if a statement is defamatory, a judge will consider the whole article and not just one sentence taken out of context.

Application to HP Facts: Had the article about Hagrid stated only that he had maimed several students, it would constitute defamation because that language suggests Hagrid intentionally hit students or otherwise purposefully caused them injury. This implication is untrue and would have hurt his reputation as a teacher.

However, the next sentence in Skeeter's article clarified the statement about maiming. It stated that Draco Malfoy was bitten by a hippogriff, and Crabbe was hurt by a flobberworm. Both are true, and the two sentences read together do not leave the impression that Hagrid intentionally hurt students. Hagrid nonetheless has grounds to be annoyed because the second statement suggests that he was not adequately monitoring the students. In fact, Hagrid had cautioned students about the creatures' tendency to nip, but Draco and Crabbe disregarded those warnings.

* * * * * * * * * * * * *

Other Areas of Law Implicated by These Facts

Freedom of the Press
Invasion of Privacy

CHAPTER 67

FALSE IMPRISONMENT

Locked Away

HP Facts: Believing that Professor Snape was about to steal the Sorcerer's Stone, Harry, Ron, and Hermione snuck out of Gryffindor Tower at night to stop him. Before they could get out of the Common Room, Neville tried to prevent them from leaving because he feared they would get caught and, yet again, lose points for Gryffindor. Hermione pointed her wand at Neville and cried, "*Petrificus Totalus*," putting him in a full Body-Bind. Neville was unable to speak, his entire body went rigid, and he was unable to move. (*SS-16*)

Additional HP Facts: Barty Crouch, Jr., with the help of Wormtail, overpowered Mad Eye Moody prior to the beginning of Harry's fourth school year. Crouch, Jr. imprisoned Moody in a magical trunk for many months. (*GOF-35*)

Additional HP Facts: Voldemort needed information from Ollivander, the wand maker, to understand the *Priori Incantem* effect when Harry's and Voldemort's wands connected. Voldemort also needed information regarding the Elder Wand. Additionally, because Luna's father was publishing in his magazine, the *Quibbler*, articles that were supportive of Harry and critical of Voldemort's Ministry agenda, Luna was taken off the Hogwarts Express by Death Eaters. Both Ollivander and Luna were held captive in the basement of Malfoy Manor. (*DH-23*)

Muggle Law: *False imprisonment* is a tort consisting of restricting a person's movements without that person's permission or authority. The same acts may constitute the crime of kidnapping.

169

Application to HP Facts: Hermione's spell on Neville resulted in his being unable to move. Although her purpose was merely to prevent Neville from stopping the threesome's departure from Gryffindor Tower, she had no right to restrain him. Her actions thus constitute false imprisonment.

Similarly, Barty Crouch, Jr. committed the tort of false imprisonment by confining Moody in the trunk. Likewise, Ollivander and Luna were falsely imprisoned in the cellar of Malfoy Manor.

* * * * * * * * * * * * *

Other Areas of Law Implicated by These Facts
Assault and Battery – The Crime
Assault and Battery – The Torts
Kidnapping

CHAPTER 68

FRAUD

How Great Am I!

HP Facts: Professor Gilderoy Lockhart wrote numerous books about his supposed adventures and exploits. He also boasted about his claimed extraordinary Wizarding abilities and courage in the face of danger. However, the true facts became apparent when the Heir of Slytherin was running loose at Hogwarts and someone was needed to enter the Chamber of Secrets to face the monster. Rather than offering assistance, Lockhart prepared to flee the castle. Harry and Ron found him busily packing his things. They could not understand why he was running away after succeeding at all the great and dangerous escapades he described in his books. Lockhart told Harry and Ron that "books can be misleading" and admitted that his books "wouldn't have sold half as well if people didn't think I'd done all those things." Harry then accused Lockhart of taking undeserved credit for what other people had done. Lockhart admitted that he picked other people's brains to learn how they managed to do what they did and then put a Memory Charm on them so they would not remember having done it. This enabled Lockhart to claim credit without anyone contradicting him. (*COS-16*)

Muggle Law: The tort of *fraud* addresses intentional deceit for personal gain. Specifically, fraud consists of the following elements:

- An untruthful statement
- Known by the speaker to be false
- The speaker's intention is to induce another person to rely on the statement and thus be misled
- At least one person does rely on it and is misled

- As a result, that person suffers a financial loss

For example, let's say I produce a CD with the music of a little-known band. I design packaging for the CD which includes a statement that the music is that of a well-known and popular rock group whose music you like a lot. You rely on the packaging and purchase the CD. When you discover the truth, you rightly want your money back. These facts constitute fraud. You would be entitled to a refund of your money.

Application to HP Facts: A big part of the public appeal of Lockhart's books was the belief that he had performed amazing magical feats entitling him to well-deserved awe and respect. In fact, he had done none of the things for which he took credit. If the buyers of his books had known the truth, they would not have purchased them. All the elements of fraud are present.

Imaginary Greatness

HP Facts: When Lockhart applied to Hogwarts for his teaching position, he likely submitted a resume to Professor Dumbledore. We can reasonably assume that his resume contained the same exaggerated and untruthful claims about his accomplishments as did his books.

Muggle Law: There is a particular type of fraud called resume fraud. It consists of misrepresenting one's credentials on a resume. The untruths can relate to professional accomplishments, college attended, degrees received, previous employers, prior job responsibilities, salary history, and more.

Application to HP Facts: Lockhart apparently lied on his resume knowing that Dumbledore would rely on the information when accessing Lockhart's qualifications for the job. By doing so, Lockhart committed resume fraud.

CHAPTER 69

INVASION OF PRIVACY

HP Facts: On the train to Harry's first year at Hogwarts, he reveled in the fact he had money for the first time in his life and someone with whom to share candy. To celebrate, he bought a variety of sweets from the lady with the candy cart. Among the goodies he bought were Bertie Bott's Every Flavor Beans, Drooble's Best Blowing Gum, Chocolate Frogs, Pumpkin Pastries, Cauldron Cakes, and Licorice Wands. When he opened one of the chocolate frogs, Harry discovered that it came with a trading card. As magic would have it, the picture on Harry's card was Professor Dumbledore's. (*SS-6*)

Muggle Law: The tort of *invasion of privacy* prohibits the use of a person's name or picture for commercial purposes unless the person has given written permission. For example, if your picture turns up on the cover of a college catalogue and you did not give authorization for its use, this would constitute the tort. The college uses the catalogue to promote its offerings and attract students, making it a commercial use.

An exception exists to this tort. The media can publish names and pictures of people who are newsworthy without the need of written permission. "Newsworthy" means of interest to the public. For example, if you won a statewide skateboarding or scrabble competition, you would be temporarily newsworthy. The media could report your accomplishment and publish your picture without needing to obtain your written permission. Another example is the President of the United States; he is newsworthy every day of his term in office.

Application to HP Facts: Combining candy with trading cards containing pictures of various people is an example of a commercial use of the photographs. The cards make the candy more desirable to kids and, thus, enhance the candy company's

173

sales. If Dumbledore had not given written permission for the use of his photo, he would have a good case for the tort of invasion of privacy.

* * * * * * * * * * * * *

Other Areas of Law Implicated by These Facts
Legal Tender

CHAPTER 70

ASSAULT AND BATTERY – THE TORTS

Brazen, Berserk Bellatrix Beats Hermione

HP Facts: After being caught by Snatchers in the woods, Harry, Ron, and Hermione were taken to Voldemort's new headquarters, Malfoy Manor. Bellatrix Lestrange and other Death Eaters were there. Bellatrix was furious that Harry, Ron, and Hermione had the sword of Gryffindor, believing they had stolen it from her vault at Gringotts Bank. After locking Harry, Ron, and others in the cellar, Bellatrix tortured Hermione for information about where she had obtained the sword. Hermione screamed repeatedly as Bellatrix used the Cruciatus Curse on her. (*DH–23*) Later, following Hermione's escape from Malfoy Manor, she recovered from the attack but, as she stood during Dobby's funeral, she was "pale and unsteady on her feet." (*DH-24*)

Additional HP Facts: The Committee for the Disposal of Dangerous Creatures ruled that Buckbeak should be executed after he injured Draco Malfoy. Thereafter, Hermione confronted Draco, furious that he had exaggerated his injuries to the Committee. Hermione marched up to Draco and slapped him hard across his face using all her strength. She would have hit Draco again, but Ron stopped her. (*POA-15*)

Muggle Law: There exists a tort of *assault* and a tort of *battery*. Each involves different conduct. The tort of battery consists of intentionally causing physical injury to another person. The tort of assault consists of intentionally committing an act that creates fear of imminent injury, such as pointing a gun.

Application to HP Facts: The Cruciatus Curse inflicts injury and excruciating pain on its victim. Bellatrix's use of the curse on Hermione constitutes the tort of battery. Concerning Draco, if Hermione's slap caused injury, her action, too, would constitute the tort of battery.

Note: It is easy to confuse the crimes and torts of assault and battery since the names are identical. However, the prohibited conduct is different. In criminal law, both terms – assault and battery – mean intentionally causing physical injury. In tort law, battery too means intentionally causing physical injury. Assault, however, means something different. It refers to conduct that intentionally puts another person in fear of imminent harmful contact but does not require that the contact occur.

* * * * * * * * * * * * *

Other Areas of Law Implicated by These Facts
Assault and Battery – The Crime
False Imprisonment
Kidnapping
Larceny
Robbery

CHAPTER 71

ASSUMPTION OF RISK

Beware the Blimey Bludger

HP Facts: J.K. Rowling introduced us to the Wizarding sport of Quidditch, which is played in the air on broomsticks. An important position on a Quidditch team is the Seeker. Harry was chosen as the Seeker for the Gryffindor team because of his superior skill at flying on a broom. Team captain Oliver Wood explained to Harry how Quidditch is played. The game includes black balls, called Bludgers, that fly at the players and try to knock them off their broomsticks. Further, each team has two Beaters who use bats to hit the Bludgers towards the opposing team members. The Beaters' objective is to dislodge the opposing team's members from their broomsticks. Harry asked if anyone had ever been killed by the Bludgers. Oliver replied that there have been broken jaws but fortunately nothing worse. (*SS-10*)

Additional HP Facts: In a Quidditch game between Gryffindor and Hufflepuff, the pompous Cormac McLaggen was substituting as Keeper, a position equivalent to goalie. He attempted to show one of his teammates the proper way to hit a Bludger. In so doing, McLaggen mistakenly hit the Bludger in Harry's direction. Harry was hit and experienced a "blinding, sickening pain" and woke up in the hospital wing with a cracked skull. (*HBP-19*)

Muggle Law: A person who knowingly engages in a dangerous sporting activity *assumes the risk*. This means if he is hurt in the normal play of the game, he is not entitled to compensation from the person who caused the injury. For example, let's say you are kicked during a soccer game by a fellow player while both of you are attempting to take control of the ball. Since your injury resulted from playing the game in

177

the customary way it is played, you would have no legal recourse.

Application to HP Facts: Once Harry became aware of how Quidditch was played, he assumed the risk that he might be injured while playing the position of Seeker. Concerning the players who suffered broken jaws, their injuries likely resulted from the ordinary course of the game. Therefore, they assumed that risk and so could not sue successfully for compensation. Since Harry's cracked skull occurred during the play of a game, he, too, assumed the risk of his injury.

Nimble Nimbus Not Normal

HP Facts: During a Quidditch match, someone (originally believed to be Professor Snape but later learned to be Professor Quirrell) put a jinx on Harry's Nimbus Two Thousand, a top-of-the-line broomstick. The spell caused it to buck, zigzag through the air, roll over repeatedly, and make violent movements that almost unseated Harry. (*SS-11*)

Muggle Law: A player does not assume the risk of dangers that are not inherent in the sport. For example, assume you are playing baseball. You are up to bat using a wooden bat. The pitch comes and your bat makes contact with the ball. Unfortunately, the bat is manufactured poorly and the impact of the hit causes the bat to shatter. A piece of the wood hits you in the face, causing injury. Since a defective bat is not a normal peril associated with playing baseball, you did not assume the risk for that type of injury. In this circumstance, you can bring a lawsuit against the manufacturer and expect to win.

Application to HP Facts: Harry did not assume the risk of any injury caused by Quirrell's jinx. The uncontrolled jerky motions the spell unleashed on Harry's broom were not part of the ordinary risks associated with Quidditch. Therefore, had

Harry been injured, he could have successfully sued Quirrell for the tort of battery.

* * * * * * * * * * * * * *

Other Areas of Law Implicated by These Facts
Assault and Battery – The Crime
Assault and Battery – The Torts
Informed Consent

CHAPTER 72

INFORMED CONSENT

Far From Feigned Fainting

HP Facts: One evening in the Gryffindor Common Room, Hermione observed Fred, George and their friend Lee Jordon sitting with a group of first year students. The newbies were chewing Fainting Fancies which Fred had provided. One by one, the students started slumping over unconscious and either slid to the floor or fell over the arms of their chairs. Fred and George were watching the students and making notes on their clipboards. Hermione attempted to put a stop to this, but Fred protested, saying they had paid the students for their participation. Hermione warned Fred and George that if they did not stop using students as guinea pigs, she would report them to Mrs. Weasley. (*OOP–13*)

Muggle Law: People sometimes agree to engage in certain conduct involving matters about which they lack knowledge and expertise. The legal concept of *informed consent* requires that people being asked to participate in a medical experiment or to consent to a medical procedure be advised of all the risks. This advice enables patients to make an educated decision about whether to participate. For example, when a person is advised by his doctor that he needs an operation, the physician must inform the patient of all the associated dangers. Only then can the patient make an informed decision about whether or not to proceed.

Application to HP Facts: Fred and George wanted to test the effects of their new product, Fainting Fancies. Given the name of the item, the twins presumably knew that the chewable pills would induce fainting-like states. The twins solicited the assistance of some first year students by offering to pay them to be guinea pigs. If the students were injured, the twins could face liability if they had failed to inform the first-years of the risks associated with the product. Mere consent by the test subjects is not enough; only informed consent would relieve Fred and George of potential liability.

* * * * * * * * * * * * *

Other Areas of Law Implicated by These Facts
Assumption of Risk

IX.

INDIVIDUAL FREEDOMS (CONSTITUTIONAL LAW, PART II)

CHAPTER 73

FREEDOM OF SPEECH

Public or Private?

HP Facts: Professor Umbridge came to Hogwarts to enforce the Ministry of Magic's agenda, which included denial that Voldemort had returned. In Harry's first Defense Against the Dark Arts class with Umbridge, Harry was outraged that she would not be teaching defensive spells. This was very troubling because Harry knew about the return of Voldemort and the Death Eaters. Harry stated to Umbridge that students needed to be prepared because Voldemort was not dead. She accused Harry of lying, docked points from Gryffindor, and gave him a week's detention. During the detentions, she forced Harry to cut into the skin on the back of his hand the words, "I must not tell lies." (*OOP-12,13*)

Muggle Law: The Constitution of the United States guarantees the right of free speech. This right means that the government cannot prevent people from expressing their views. The right exists whether the opinion is shared by many, is unpopular, not "politically correct," or even biased and mean-spirited. However, the right of free speech does have limits. For example, you cannot make untrue statements about others (that could be defamation), incite people to riot, or otherwise create an immediate risk to public safety, such as yelling "fire" in a public movie theater (unless, of course, there is a fire).

Public Schools. Principals and teachers in public schools are considered to be government representatives. The right of free speech thus applies to students in public schools. However, the law recognizes that schools have to maintain order and discipline, and so school officials are allowed under certain circumstances to limit students' right to speak out. For a public school to limit student expression, the message must significantly disrupt the work and discipline of the school.

An example of free speech activity in a school is a student who wears a black armband as a form of protest against a war. This form of protest will not likely cause a substantial disruption of the school's activities. Therefore, the school could not prevent the student from displaying the armband. Another example relates to students who create websites that express an opinion such as complaints about a teacher or cafeteria food. This is protected free speech and does not disrupt the school's operations. Any discipline of the students would violate their constitutional rights.

The type of free speech activity a public school can prohibit includes student speeches to the student body using sexually-explicit or otherwise indecent language. Likewise, the school can bar student comments that encourage others to break the law.

Private Schools. The right of free speech in the federal Constitution prohibits only the *government* from suppressing speech. Private schools do not receive government money. Administrators and faculty at such schools are not government officials and so the federal constitutional right of free speech does not bar censorship. In some states, protection of free speech for private school students exists and is grounded in one of several sources – the *state* constitution or a *state* statute. Additionally some private schools may have adopted a policy granting students a right of free speech.

Application to HP Facts: The status of Hogwarts as a public or private school is not clear. If we assume that Hogwarts is a *private* school, the right of free speech would not apply. Therefore, Hogwarts would not be required to honor students' free speech rights unless they are granted in some other law or policy at the state or school level. We know of no such policy applicable at Hogwarts.

During Umbridge's year at the school, the Ministry of Magic dictated many of the rules. It blindly refused to acknowledge Voldemort's return and ruthlessly squelched all comments suggesting he might be back again. Although Harry was frustrated by Umbridge's refusal to let him discuss Voldemort's status, if the school is private, Umbridge was not violating Harry's constitutional right.

If we assume that Hogwarts is a *public* school, the Ministry would argue it was justified in suppressing Harry's comments. Its argument would be that the references to Voldemort's reappearance would cause much fear among students, and therefore significantly disrupt the work and discipline of the school.

* * * * * * * * * * * * * *

Other Areas of Law Implicated by These Facts
Corporal Punishment
In Loco Parentis

CHAPTER 74

FREEDOM OF THE PRESS

Extra Extra

HP Facts: The daily newspaper that reports on the Wizarding world is the *Daily Prophet*. This paper also has an evening addition called the *Evening Prophet*. The Ministry of Magic under Cornelius Fudge influenced the newspaper both to refrain from reporting that Voldemort had returned and to publish articles to discredit Harry and Dumbledore. Hermione believed it was important for Harry to tell his side of the story regarding the return of Voldemort and the death of Cedric Diggory. She arranged for Rita Skeeter to interview Harry, and for Luna Lovegood's father, the editor of the magazine the *Quibbler*, to publish the article. After it appeared in the *Quibbler*, Professor Umbridge was furious. She took points from Gryffindor and gave Harry detention. Further, as High Inquisitor of Hogwarts, she issued an order prohibiting students from reading the *Quibbler* and announced that any student found in possession of the magazine would be expelled. (*OOP-26*)

Additional HP Facts: Luna Lovegood's father, Xenophilius, is the publisher of a magazine called the *Quibbler*. Following Voldemort's takeover of the Ministry, the *Quibbler* published articles supportive of Harry and critical of the Ministry and Voldemort. The new regime refused to tolerate such commentary, so the Death Eaters kidnapped Luna. She was held hostage to force Xenophilius to change the opinions he published. In a bid to secure Luna's release, the *Quibbler* printed an edition that featured a picture of Harry labeled as Undesirable Number One and an announcement of a reward that was being offered for his capture. (*DH-21*)

Muggle Law: The Constitution of the United States guarantees freedom of the press. The term "press" is broader than just newspapers and includes all means of mass communication – radio, TV, the Internet, and You Tube. Freedom of the press means that all people have the right both to convey their opinions via the media and to receive a variety of ideas without interference from the government. Neither publishers nor reporters can be punished for circulating opinions, regardless of how critical they may be of government and regardless of the fact they deviate from the government's official position on a topic. Rather, the press is free from control by the state, and journalists are free from retaliation by the government.

In a society that lacks freedom of the press, the government controls the media. This means the government determines the content of the news. In these societies, government uses the media to restrict and control people's access to information and opposing views. The media is also used to indoctrinate the public on official positions of the government concerning issues of the day. Opinions that deviate are not tolerated. People who write or publish unapproved information or views are considered traitors. They face intimidation, threats, kidnapping, torture or assassination.

Application to HP Facts: Because the United States enjoys freedom of the press, the Ministry would not be able to control the content of newspapers or other media. Instead, the Internet, radio, TV, and newspapers can publish any and all news and views without fear of retribution. J.K. Rowling accurately portrays the impact of government control of the media. The vast majority of the Wizarding world did not know that Voldemort had returned. Anyone who suggested he had reappeared and regained power was brutally punished. For example, the kidnapping of Xenophilius' daughter Luna was retaliation for what he printed in the *Quibbler*, supporting Harry.

* * * * * * * * * * * * *

Other Areas of Law Implicated by These Facts
Corporal Punishment
False Imprisonment
Freedom of Speech
Kidnapping

CHAPTER 75

FREEDOM OF ASSEMBLY

The DA DOA

HP Facts: Harry, Ron, and Hermione were concerned that they were not learning anything useful in Defense Against the Dark Arts from Professor Umbridge. They decided to have a meeting at the Hogs Head bar in Hogsmead Village with other Hogwarts students who might be interested in learning more. This group ultimately formed the DA (Dumbledore's Army). Unfortunately, while having their initial meeting at the Hogs Head, they were overheard, and the gathering of students was reported to Umbridge. Consequently, she arranged for the Ministry of Magic to issue Educational Decree No. 24 which banned "all student organizations, societies, teams and clubs" at Hogwarts and precluded them from re-forming or existing in the future without her permission. (*OOP-16,17,27*)

Muggle Law: The Federal Constitution provides for freedom of assembly, the right to associate with and organize groups, gatherings, clubs, or organizations without interference from the government. This right entitles us to form or join any special interest group, political party, union or other organization we might like for the purpose of sharing our views and interests with like-minded people. The government cannot restrict us from doing so. Freedom of assembly also protects our right to protest with others against circumstances we find offensive. These may include, for example, environmental pollution, the minimum drinking age, civil rights, privacy on the Internet, or war. Without freedom of assembly, the government could ban public protests of any kind, as well as groups whose missions do not agree with positions of the government and political parties that oppose the current administration.

Not all gatherings are protected. Freedom of assembly protects peaceful, orderly, gatherings and demonstrations. Sometimes groups become quite zealous in advancing their cause, and protestors can become unruly. Freedom of assembly does not protect gatherings that threaten public safety.

Freedom of Assembly at School. Private schools are not part of the government so they are not bound by the right of freedom of assembly. A private school can therefore prohibit students from coming together to share and promote common beliefs.

Public schools are funded at least in part by the government so they are considered a part of the government. Therefore, their ability to restrict student clubs and organizations is limited by freedom of assembly. However, schools have a duty to maintain the wellbeing of all its students. The upshot is this: Students have a right to demonstrate on public school property. However the protest must be reasonable as to the time of day it occurs, location on campus, and behavior of the participants. If the gathering significantly disrupts classes or school business (such as blocking the entry or exit from buildings), disrupts school activities (for example, is so loud that other students cannot hear their teachers in classes), or if it creates substantial disorder, the school can stop it.

Application of HP Facts: The DA was not disrupting any Hogwarts activity or interfering with the comings and goings of students who were not involved with the group. The status of Hogwarts as a public or private school is not clear. If Hogwarts is a public school, Educational Decree No. 24 would be null and void; it could not prevent the DA from meeting. If, however, Hogwarts is a private school, it could indeed prevent students from meeting, even peaceably. The Decree in that circumstance would be enforceable.

* * * * * * * * * * * * * *

Other Areas of Law Implicated by These Facts

Freedom of Speech
In Loco Parentis

CHAPTER 76

EQUAL PROTECTION

Winky, Wands, and Werewolfs

HP Facts: At the World Quidditch Cup Tournament, Winky the house elf was found with Harry's wand following the appearance of the Dark Mark in the sky. The Code of Wands states that, "No non-human creature is permitted to carry or use a wand." (*GOF-9*)

Additional HP Facts: At the headquarters of the Order of the Phoenix, Hermione had a conversation with Lupin concerning her views on elf rights. She commented about the "nonsense of werewolf segregation . . . this horrible thing wizards have of thinking they're superior to other creatures." We know from earlier parts of the story that werewolves such as Lupin are looked down upon in Wizard society and are often the victims of discrimination. (*OOP-9*)

Additional HP Facts: Following the takeover of the Ministry of Magic by Voldemort, the Muggle-born Registration Commission was formed. This Commission required all Muggle-borns (witches or wizards with non-magical parents) to register with the Ministry and to present themselves before the Commission to be interviewed. The stated purpose was to ensure they did not obtain their magical powers by theft. Unless the Muggle-born witch or wizard could prove magical ancestry, they could be sent to Azkaban Prison on suspicion of theft. Additionally, unless students could prove their Blood Status, they were prohibited from attending Hogwarts. (*DH-11*)

Muggle Law: Unfortunately, our country's past includes an unproud history of discrimination against minorities.

Government and businesses both supported a system of segregation and inferior treatment. A practice known as *separate but equal* had justified separate and typically inferior facilities for use by minorities for decades. This abusive conduct and forced segregation occurred notwithstanding a provision in our Federal Constitution that prohibits government from denying to any person the "equal protection of the laws."

An important development occurred in 1954 – the United States Supreme Court case of *Brown v. Board of Education*. That decision outlawed the rule of separate but equal. Another significant advancement was the Civil Rights Act of 1964 (the "Act") which barred certain businesses from refusing service to minority customers. The goal of the Act was to recognize the value of all people and enable everyone to benefit from the services provided by certain businesses.

Specifically, the Act outlaws discrimination by restaurants, hotels, places of amusement (beaches, theaters, etc.), and gas stations. The categories for which the Act prohibits discrimination are race, color of skin, religion, and nationality. Gender was added in 1990. Other federal, state and local laws prohibit discrimination based on disability, marital status, and, in some states, sexual orientation. Various states protect additional traits. Together these categories of people are called *protected classes*. Sadly, many businesses resisted integration even after passage of the Act. Nonetheless, the referenced Supreme Court case and the Act were important advancements for race relations. They heralded a new, but unfortunately hard-fought, era of increased access for all.

* * * * * * * * * * * * * *

Other Areas of Law Implicated by These Facts
Abolition of Slavery
Evidence

CHAPTER 77

ABOLITION OF SLAVERY

Dobby Does Dishes

HP Facts: Throughout the series, we encounter numerous house elves including Dobby, Winky and Kreacher. A house elf's status is akin to slavery. House elves are owned by a Wizarding family and are bound to serve them for life, catering to their every whim. Elves who speak ill of the family or act contrary to the family's interest must physically punish themselves. We painfully observe Dobby beating his head against a wall on several occasions. Hermione is to be applauded for her efforts to upgrade their conditions through S.P.E.W., The Society for the Protection of Elfish Welfare. There is one way only that house elves can be freed – if their master gives them clothing. (*COS-10*)

Muggle Law: During an unproud time in the history of the United States, before the Civil War, the law authorized slavery. Slave traders went to Africa, kidnapped people, brought them to this country in boats ill-equipped for the long journey, and sold them as slaves, primarily to plantation owners in the south. The slaves became property of their purchasers. The slaves planted and picked crops, performed physical labor as needed on the farm, cooked and served food, cared for their owner and his family, and did whatever else was needed to maintain the homestead.

Slaves were not paid for their services except they received room and food which were typically meager and substandard. Slaves were subjected to beatings and whippings with little or no provocation, forced to work long hours under oppressive conditions, shamelessly exploited, and often separated from their family members who were sold to different owners. If

194

any slaves tried to escape, their owner could legally retrieve them by force. Since they were recognized as property, law enforcement aided owners in searching for missing slaves. Upon return, the runaway slave was severely punished, in part to discourage other slaves from attempting to leave.

The southern states greatly benefited from slavery. The warmer weather rendered farming an important enterprise. The north, with its colder weather and emphasis less on crops and more on industry, was less reliant on slave labor and questioned its morality. The lines were drawn and a Civil War was fought beginning in 1861. Two years later in 1863, President Abraham Lincoln issued the Emancipation Proclamation, an order freeing all slaves in the south. The Confederacy, as the coalition of southern states was known, surrendered in 1865. The war was followed by the Thirteenth Amendment to the United States Constitution which reads, "Neither slavery nor involuntary servitude . . . shall exist within the United States . . .."

Application to HP Facts: Fortunately today, a family utilizing the services of house elves or other servants would not be able to treat them as slaves. Rather, the family would be required to be respectful and comply with existing laws that protect domestic workers.

* * * * * * * * * * * * * *

Other Areas of Law Implicated by These Facts
Employment Issues

195

CHAPTER 78

GUN CONTROL

Firearms Trigger Restrictions

HP Facts: In the very beginning of the Harry Potter story, Hogwarts School of Witchcraft and Wizardry tried to deliver a letter to Harry notifying him that he was accepted to attend. Uncle Vernon refused to let Harry read the mail. Owls then flooded the Dursley house with letters. To escape, Uncle Vernon took the family to a shack on a large rock in the sea. He took a rifle with him that he displayed when Hagrid began banging on the door. (*SS-4*)

Additional HP Facts: After Sirius Black escaped from Azkaban Prison, the *Daily Prophet* reported that Black had a gun. The article described the gun as a "kind of metal wand that Muggles use to kill each other." (*POA-3*)

Muggle Law: Guns can easily cause death. To protect the public, many restrictions exist on the sale and possession of firearms. These limitations are imposed by both federal and state law. Some avid gun owners argue that the restrictions violate the Second Amendment to the Federal Constitution which reads as follows, "A well regulated militia, being necessary to the security of a free state, the right of the people to keep and bear Arms, shall not be infringed." This dispute is ongoing and courts are reviewing the issue.

The two most significant federal statutes controlling possession and sale of firearms outside the military are the National Firearms Act of 1934 and the Gun Control Act of 1968. Among the requirements imposed by these statutes is that a business selling firearms must first obtain a federal firearms license. Further, handguns cannot be sold to anyone under age 21. Likewise, long guns (such as rifles) cannot be sold to anyone under age 18. Before transferring a gun to any buyer, sellers are required to verify two facts: (1) the identity of the purchaser by inspecting a government-issued form of ID, such as a driver's license and (2) the eligibility of the buyer to possess a firearm. This involves a record check with a system operated by the Federal Bureau of Investigation (FBI) designed to inform the seller within 30 seconds whether the proposed sale would violate federal law.

Nine categories of people are prohibited from possessing firearms. Among them are people convicted of a crime punishable by more than a year in jail (generally speaking, a felony), fugitives from justice, drug users or addicts, and persons declared by a judge to be mentally incompetent or who are committed to a mental institution. A would-be buyer who is denied on any of these grounds can appeal the decision.

Most states have additional restrictions on the purchase, sale, and possession of firearms. Sales initiated through the Internet are subject to the same laws as sales made in person.

Application to HP Facts: If Uncle Vernon or Sirius Black (if he had a gun which, in fact, he did not) obtained their guns illegally, they and their sellers could face prosecution and penalties.

The record check on Black, however, would have revealed that he was a fugitive from justice rendering him ineligible to purchase.

* * * * * * * * * * * * * *

Other Areas of Law Implicated by These Facts
Mail Abuse
Murder

CHAPTER 79

MARTIAL LAW

Loss of Liberties

HP Facts: During the initial reign of terror of Lord Voldemort, the Ministry of Magic went to great lengths to capture Voldemort's supporters. The law of the Wizarding world contained a strict prohibition against the use of the Unforgivable Curses. During Voldemort's first reign, the Ministry modified the prohibition to permit the use of Unforgivable Curses against his followers. Also during this time, Aurors were given the authority not to just capture Voldemort's supporters but to kill them on sight without a trial to verify their guilt. In the alternative, Aurors were permitted to hand over suspected supporters to the dementors who would take Voldemort's henchmen directly to Azkaban Prison without a trial. For example, Sirius Black, believed to be a Death Eater, was captured and sent directly to Azkaban where he remained for 12 years. After his escape, the Ministry gave the dementors the authority to "perform the Kiss" on Sirius if and when recaptured. Since the Kiss sucks out a person's soul, this is the equivalent of death, or worse. Had Black been afforded a trial, he might have proven his innocence. (*GOF-27, POA-12*)

Muggle Law: In the event of a national, state or local emergency, the government can temporarily suspend laws and direct the military to take control. The purpose of such drastic action is to eliminate chaos and secure order. The system of rules used by the military in such circumstances is called *martial law*. Usually martial law results in a suspension of civil rights. The effects can include imposition of stricter penalties for outlawed conduct and authorization of the death penalty for certain crimes even if the law does not ordinarily permit the death penalty, or even recognize the action as criminal. Martial law also curtails the right of a jail inmate to contest the legality of his imprisonment, a right called *habeas corpus*. A curfew may be imposed limiting the right to freely come and go.

Martial law can be invoked only in limited circumstances where the existing authorities are unable to maintain public order. These include major public emergencies such as a terrorist attack, a natural disaster, an epidemic of a contagious disease, or other serious public health emergency. For example, in New Orleans, Louisiana, following the flooding of that city that resulted from Hurricane Katrina in 2005, the mayor declared a state of emergency. Federal troops and National Guardsmen were brought in to patrol the city to prevent looting and chaos. Many civil rights were temporarily suspended.

Application to HP Facts: Voldermort's reign of terror is akin to a terrorist attack or enemy invasion. It is exactly the type of circumstance that could justify the use of martial law. To aid in the apprehension of Voldemort and his cronies, and thereby end the serious threat to the public as soon as possible, the Ministry acted legally when it imposed a martial law-like suspension of liberties.

* * * * * * * * * * * * *

Other Areas of Law Implicated by These Facts
Death Penalty
Emergency Restrictions
Innocent Until Proven Guilty
Notice and Opportunity to be Heard

199

X.

CONTRACTS

CHAPTER 80

FREEDOM OF CONTRACT

Triwizard Tournament and the Binding Magical

HP Facts: Eligible students from the three magical schools – Hogwarts, Beauxbatons and Durmstrang – who wanted to compete in the Triwizard Tournament could apply by writing their name on a piece of parchment and putting it in the Goblet of Fire. Only one student from each school customarily participated. The students were warned that once a competitor was selected from the names submitted, he or she was obligated to compete from beginning to end of the tournament. Professor Dumbledore made it clear that "placing your name in the goblet constitutes a binding magical contract" and warned that students should be sure about their interest before submitting their name. After Harry's name was drawn from the Goblet, he was bound to compete even though he was not the one who submitted his name and even though he did not want to participate. (*GOF-16*)

Muggle Law: A *contract* is a binding agreement between two or more parties who each agree to either give something to the other or do something for the other. The legal significance of a contract is that if one party fails to perform (this is called *breach of contract*), the other is entitled to a remedy. The usual remedy is money to compensate for any loss incurred as a result of the breach. For the contract to be binding, both parties must enter it voluntarily, agree to its terms, and be over the age of 18 years. The United States Constitution contains a right to *freedom of contract*. This means everyone is entitled to enter a contract as well as refuse to enter a contract, as each person sees fit without interference from the government.

Application to HP Facts: By putting their name in the Goblet, students entered a "binding magical contract" that required them to compete in the Tournament if chosen. The time for students to decide whether or not they wanted to

201

compete was *before* submitting their name. However, in the Muggle world, Harry would not be bound to participate because he was not the one who submitted his name, and he did not voluntarily agree to participate. Further, he was not old enough to enter a binding contract.

$$* * * * * * * * * * * * * *$$

Other Areas of Law Implicated by These Facts
Forgery
Restrictions on Minors

CHAPTER 81

CONSIDERATION

I Promise

HP Facts: Harry needed Uncle Vernon to sign a permission form before Harry could join other students on occasional weekend field trips to the Village of Hogsmead to shop. Harry made a bargain with Uncle Vernon that Harry would act "normal" while Aunt Marge was visiting if Uncle Vernon would sign the form. (*POA-2*)

Additional HP Facts: Harry and Hermione organized the DA (Dumbledore's Army) so Harry could teach, and the members could learn, about Defense Against the Dark Arts. The organization was formed because students were not learning much from Professor Umbridge. At the first meeting of the DA, Hermione suggested that all the members sign their name on a piece of parchment evidencing their agreement not to tell Umbridge or anyone else what they were doing. "There was an odd feeling in the group now. It was as though they had just signed some kind of contract." (*OOP-16*)

Muggle Law: To be valid, a contract requires something the law calls *consideration*. The word's use with contracts is different from the meaning we normally associate with the word. Rather than "thoughtfulness of others" or "careful reflection," the term when associated with contracts refers to something exchanged for something else. Consideration can take one of three forms – something of value, an act, or forbearance (refraining from doing something you have a legal right to do). Additionally, consideration includes a promise to give something of value, do an act, or forbear.

An example of consideration's being something of value is as follows: You go to the store to buy a pair of jeans and select the pair you want. You cannot just walk out of the store with them. Instead, you must give the clerk money in return. The money is the consideration for the jeans. Similarly, the jeans are consideration for the money.

Application to HP Facts: In the bargain Harry made with his uncle, the consideration for Uncle Vernon granting permission for Harry to visit Hogsmead is Harry's promise to act normally in the presence of Aunt Marge. Uncle Vernon's promised consideration was an act (signing the permission slip), and Harry's consideration was forbearance (refraining from acting weird or displaying any magic).

Harry and the members of the DA each gave consideration in the form of forbearance. Since each had the right to inform Umbridge or anyone else of the goings-on of the DA, each of their promises to refrain from doing so constitutes consideration for the others' promises to likewise remain mum.

* * * * * * * * * * * * * *

Other Areas of Law Implicated by These Facts
Freedom of Contract
In Loco Parentis
Restrictions on Minors

CHAPTER 82

WRITTEN AND ORAL AGREEMENTS

A Big Deal that Got Away

HP Facts: Uncle Vernon worked for a company that made drills. He was hoping for a large order from a customer who was a rich builder and invited the customer to dinner at the Dursleys' home. Harry's uncle was very concerned that everything go exactly right so the builder would be inclined to enter a contract to purchase many drills. Uncle Vernon announced to his family, "This could well be the day I make the biggest deal of my career . . .. With any luck I'll have the deal signed and sealed before the news at ten." He told them he would use the money to buy a summer home in Majorca, a popular tourist destination. *(COS-1)*

Muggle Law: As a general rule, oral contracts are binding on the parties. However, certain types of contracts must be in writing and signed to be enforceable. One such contract is sale of merchandise over the amount of $500.00 (amendments have been proposed to raise this amount to $5,000.00). Among the other contracts requiring a writing, are sale of land and buildings and agreements that will take more than a year to perform.

Application to HP Facts: Uncle Vernon was hoping to enter a contract with his dinner guest for a large sum of money. The contract would have required Uncle Vernon to provide a quantity of drills (indeed, he was hoping it would be a very large quantity) and the builder to pay for them. The cost to the builder would likely have been significantly more than $500.00. Therefore, the contract would have required a writing and the parties' signatures. Uncle Vernon referenced the agreement being "signed and sealed." In earlier times, companies often had an official seal that was stamped on its

205

contracts to indicate agreement to the contract terms. Seals are seldom used anymore in this country. A signature of a party who has the necessary authority is sufficient to bind the company.

But for Dobby, the house elf, Uncle Vernon would probably be spending summers in Majorca. However, the sounds of Dobby talking, a spell on Aunt Petunia's "masterpiece of a pudding," and the arrival at the Dursleys of an owl with a letter just as the diners were finishing their meal, put an end to Uncle Vernon's vacation plans.

* * * * * * * * * * * * *

Other Areas of Law Implicated by These Facts
Freedom of Contract

CHAPTER 83

WARRANTIES

Wand Warrants Weighty Warranty

HP Fact: When Harry purchased his wand at *Ollivander's: Makers of Fine Wands since 382 B.C.*, Mr. Ollivander commented, "Every Ollivander wand has a core of a powerful, magical substance. We use unicorn hairs, phoenix tail feathers, and the heartstrings of dragons." (*SS-5*)

Muggle Law: When a seller makes statements about an item he is selling, a warranty may be created. A warranty, which is sometimes called a guarantee, is a seller's pledge that the good will perform to certain standards or have the qualities described. To create a warranty, the seller's statement must assert a verifiable fact and be part of what induced the buyer to buy. If the good does not perform consistent with the guarantee or is misrepresented, seller has breached the warranty. This entitles the buyer to reimbursement from the seller for any loss buyer may incur as a result of the breach or to return the item for a refund.

Puffing. An exception to warranty law is something called *puffing*. These are statements that are obvious exaggerations or opinions of the speaker. Puffing does not create a warranty.

Application to HP Facts: The statements made by Mr. Ollivander about Harry's wand included verifiable facts and, thus, created warranties. The warranty would be breached in any of the following circumstances: (1) the wand lacked a powerful magic substance as its core; (2) the hairs were not from a unicorn; (3) the feathers were not from a phoenix; (4) the phoenix feathers were not tail feathers; (5) the wand did not contain heartstrings of dragons; or (6) another wand existed identical to Harry's. Had any of the statements been false, Harry would be entitled either to return the wand for a refund or to receive compensation from Mr. Ollivander representing the resulting reduction in the wand's value.

An example of puffing would be if Mr. Ollivander had said, "These are the best wands in the world." This is obviously a statement of Mr. Ollivander's opinion and so does not create a warranty. If Harry had found a wand he liked better from a competitor, he could not sue Ollivander for breach of warranty.

* * * * * * * * * * * * *

Other Areas of Law Implicated by These Facts
Freedom of Contract

XI.

MISCELLANEOUS TOPICS

CHAPTER 84

WILLS AND INHERITANCE

Where There's No Will, There's Still a Way

HP Facts: Before his first year at Hogwarts, Harry needed money to buy school books, robes, a wand, a cauldron, scales, a telescope, and other supplies. In a quandary about how to pay for them, he was relieved to learn from Hagrid that Harry's parents left him money located at Gringotts Bank in Diagon Alley. Hagrid took Harry to his vault at the bank where Harry withdrew some of the money to pay for his school supplies. *(SS-5)*

Additional HP Facts: The Headquarters for the Order of the Phoenix is a house located at Number Twelve Grimmauld Place. We learn that the building is owned by Sirius Black. As the last surviving Black family member, Sirius inherited the house, all of its contents, and the house elf Kreacher, apparently from his mother. *(OOP-5)*

Muggle Law: The law allows us to choose who we want to have our possessions after we die. We record our intentions in a document called a *will*. Not everyone has a will. Sometimes people just do not get around to writing one. J.K Rowling never tells us whether Harry's parents had a will. There is a legal term that means a person died without a will. That term is *intestate*. When people die intestate their possessions go to relatives designated by state law. While the beneficiaries vary somewhat from state to state, typically intestate laws distribute property as follows:

- If the deceased (the person who dies) has children and a spouse, the property is divided among them in proportions that vary depending on the number of children.
- If the deceased has a spouse but no children, the spouse takes all.

210

- If the deceased has children but no spouse, the children take all.
- If the deceased has no spouse and no children, the property passes to the next closest relative.

Application to HP Facts: Since both of Harry's parents passed away, and Harry was their only child, he is entitled to all their assets including, the money in the vault at Gringotts.

When Sirius' mother died, her husband apparently was no longer alive. Her property would therefore pass to her children. She had two children, Sirius and Regulus. Had Regulus been alive, he and Sirius would have each been entitled to half of their mother's property. Since Regulus died before his mother, Sirius takes all.

A Will Will Honor Your Will

HP Facts: Following Sirius' death, Harry learns that Sirius had a will. In it he bequeathed (gave in a will) to Harry all of Sirius' property, including gold (which Harry adds to his bank account), the house at Number Twelve Grimmauld Place, the house elf Kreacher, and Buckbeak the hippogriff. (*HBP-3*)

Additional HP Facts: Following the death of Professor Dumbledore, Minister of Magic Rufus Scrimgeour arrives at the Burrow to speak with Harry, Ron, and Hermione about Dumbledore's will. In it, Dumbledore bequeathed to Ron the Deluminator, to Hermione, the book, *The Tales of Beedle the Bard*, and to Harry, the first Snitch that he caught in his first Quidditch match and the sword of Godric Griffindor. When Harry asked why Scrimgeour waited more than a month before telling them about the will and the bequests, Scrimgeour stated that The Decree for Justifiable Confiscation gives the Ministry of Magic the power to confiscate certain property referenced in a will. Hermione then explained that the Decree "was created to stop wizards from passing Dark artifacts." Further, the

"Ministry is supposed to have powerful evidence that the deceased's possessions are illegal before seizing them." She also explained that the law provides the Ministry only 31 days to make such a determination before it is required to turn over to the beneficiaries the items referenced in the will. If the possessions prove to be dangerous, however, the Ministry can retain them. (*DH-7*)

Muggle Law: By making a will, we can select anyone we want to receive our possessions. We can leave all of our goods to one person or we can mix and match. Maybe a friend has always told you how much she loves your portable keyboard. If you wish, you can designate her to receive that instrument and leave other possessions to someone else. You can also leave money or property to a charitable organization. For example, Hermione, in her will, might want to make a donation to S.P.E.W., The Society for the Protection of Elfish Welfare. After death, a court will review the will, confirm its validity, and distribute the property as it directs. This process is called *probate*. If any illegal possessions are discovered, the court will confiscate them and likely destroy them.

Application to HP Facts: Because Sirius wrote a will and named Harry as the beneficiary, Harry will receive all of Sirius' property. Such is the power of a will.

Had Sirius not had a will, Harry would not have inherited any of his property because Harry is not a relative and only relatives benefit when a person dies intestate. While Sirius was Harry's godfather, that relationship does not qualify.

Concerning Dumbledore's will, following probate, Harry, Ron and Hermione would be entitled to the items Dumbledore designated unless they proved to be illegal.

Thy Will Be Done

HP Facts: Dumbledore told Harry that Black family tradition required that the house be handed down in the Black bloodline to the next male family member with the name of Black. We know that Sirius' younger brother Regulus had died before Sirius and Regulus had no children. Therefore, Sirius was the last male family member with the name of Black. (*HBP-3*)

Muggle Law: A will takes priority over family tradition.

Application to HP Facts: Even if a male in the Black family had survived Sirius, the house would nonetheless pass to Harry per Sirius' direction in his will.

All Are Welcome

HP Facts: Another concern of Dumbledore was that there might be an "enchantment" that would prohibit the house's being owned by anyone not a "pureblood" witch or wizard. (Reminder: Harry's mom was Muggle-born.) (*HBP-3*)

Muggle Law: When separate but equal was the accepted practice in race relations in the United States, discrimination against minorities was, sadly, rampant. One aspect of the discrimination related to the purchase and sale of homes. People of certain races and color were often denied the opportunity to purchase houses in desirable neighborhoods. This practice was justified by provisions in *deeds,* the documents that evidence ownership in houses and land. These provisions are called *restrictive covenants.* They stated that any purported sale of the property to specified minorities was void and so not recognized in law. Today, these types of restrictions are, very appropriately, illegal and unenforceable.

Application to HP Facts: Any attempted restriction on the transfer of property that would limit new owners to certain races or "purebloods" would not be enforceable.

* * * * * * * * * * * * * *

Other Areas of Law Implicated by These Facts
Abolition of Slavery
Legal Tender
Murder

CHAPTER 85

BURIAL AND GRAVE ISSUES

Wormtail Proves Very Handy; Dumbledore's Death Disturbed

HP Facts: At the end of the Triwizard Tournament, Harry mastered the maze and found the winner's cup. As he and Cedric Diggory touched it, they learned too late that it was a Portkey. They were instantly transported to a graveyard where Voldemort's father, Tom Riddle, Sr., was buried. Wormtail arrived carrying a bundle that contained all that remained of Voldemort. Sadly, Wormtail killed Cedric. Wormtail then conjured ropes that he used to bind Harry to Riddle's tombstone. Voldemort's servant then took dust from a bone in Riddle's grave as part of the spell to restore Voldemort. (*GOF-32*)

Additional HP Facts: Voldemort believed that if he possessed the Elder Wand, he would be unbeatable. He learned that Professor Dumbledore's wand was, in fact, the Elder Wand and was buried with him following his death. Voldemort went to Dumbledore's tomb in the grounds of Hogwarts, split it open, and took the Elder Wand from Dumbledore's grasp. (*DH-24*)

Muggle Law: Many states have laws prohibiting damage to cemeteries and burial plots. Numerous states also have statutes criminalizing removal or disturbance of human remains.

Application to HP Facts: By removing the bone dust from the grave of Tom Riddle, Wormtail violated the laws that prohibit vandalizing human remains. He could be prosecuted for commission of that crime. Likewise, Voldemort disturbed Dumbledore's remains and damaged his tomb. Voldermort too would be guilty of criminal conduct.

215

* * * * * * * * * * * * * *

Other Areas of Law Implicated by These Facts

Criminal Mischief/Vandalism
False Imprisonment
Kidnapping
Murder

CHAPTER 86

EMPLOYMENT ISSUES

Nose to Grindstone

HP Facts: Hermione learned from Nearly Headless Nick that Hogwarts has the largest number of house elves in Britain, over one hundred. The house elves work in the kitchens all day and then come out at night to do cleaning, light fires, and other work. Hermione is flabbergasted to learn that the house elves do not get paid, do not get holidays off, and do not receive any sick leave or pension. (*GOF-12*)

Muggle Law: Historically, many employers have abused employees, requiring that they work long hours in unsafe environments for little pay. Over time, many laws have been adopted that protect employees from ill-treatment and exploitation by employers.

Minimum and Overtime Pay. An example of laws that now protect employees is the Fair Labor Standards Act (FLSA). It requires that most employees in the United States be paid at least a minimum hourly wage. In addition, it requires that many workers receive overtime pay, meaning extra money for working more than 40 hours in a week. The required pay for working overtime is one-and-one-half times the regular pay. So, if an employee earns $8.00 per hour, she is entitled to $12.00 for each hour worked in excess of 40 hours in a given week.

Paid Sick Leave. Sick leave refers to an employer's paying an employee while the latter is unable to work due to illness. No federal or state law requires that employers provide paid sick leave. A few cities have ordinance that mandate it. Nonetheless, many employers provide this benefit. Some require a doctor's note to verify the illness.

Unpaid Sick Leave. Sometimes an employee has a lengthy medical problem or needs to care for a close relative who is ill. Additional unpaid leave may be available under a law called the Family and Medical Leave Act. This statute states that employers with 50 or more employees must provide qualifying workers up to 12 weeks of unpaid leave a year for certain personal or family medical reasons.

Paid Holidays and Vacations. No law requires that an employer provide paid holidays or paid vacations. Nonetheless, most employers do provide these benefits. Those that do not are quite rare and, no doubt, have difficulty attracting workers.

Paid holidays customarily include New Year's Day, Memorial Day, Fourth of July, Labor Day, Thanksgiving, and Christmas. Other holidays that some employers give as paid days are Martin Luther King Day, Presidents' Day, Good Friday, and Veterans Day. Many companies also allow employees to take a paid day off for their birthday.

Most employers increase the amount of paid vacation as the employee's tenure with the company grows. The most common amount is two weeks after 1 year of service, three weeks after 5 years, four weeks after 10 or 15 years, and five weeks after 25 years.

Pensions. A pension is money paid to an employee following retirement. Employers are not required to provide pensions, however, many employers do. To fund them, the employer sets aside money on a regular basis while the employee is working. Numerous laws have been adopted to ensure that the money is invested soundly and that employees receive their pensions as promised.

Unions. The law recognizes that individual workers' bargaining power with their employers is quite limited. When employees work together to achieve greater benefits, their chances of success is significantly improved. The law authorizes workers to form unions, which are organizations that negotiate with employers for improved pay, benefits and working conditions.

Domestic Service Workers. Several states and localities have recognized that Domestic workers (these include housekeeper, chauffeurs, cooks, and full-time baby sitters) are too often subject to abuse. The reasons for this include that they are isolated from their fellow employees, they may be illegal immigrants, they are frequently expected to work long hours, and they often do not speak English well. Laws have been proposed in some states and counties called Domestic Workers' Bill of Rights. In 2010, New York became the first state to adopt such a law. It requires employers to pay domestic workers one and one-half times their regular hourly wage for all hours worked in excess of 40. It also requires the employer to give one full day of rest to the worker every week.

Many organizations akin to Hermione's S.P.E.W. (Society for the Protection of Elfish Welfare) have advocated for the passage of such laws.

Application to HP Facts: If the house elves lived in the Muggle world, they would be protected against exploitation by a variety of employment laws that would impact and significantly improve their pay, hours of work, and terms of employment.

* * * * * * * * * * * * * *

Other Areas of Law Implicated by These Facts
Abolition of Slavery
Legal Tender

CHAPTER 87

VETERANS' BENEFITS

Protecting the Protectors

HP Facts: Neville Longbottom's parents were Aurors in the service of the Ministry of Magic and were captured by Death Eaters. The Death Eaters believed that Mr. and Mrs. Longbottom knew Voldemort's whereabouts and tortured them to obtain the information. Angered because the Longbottom's failed to provide it, the Death Eaters performed the Cruciatus Curse on them. As a result, both became insane. Their care is provided by St. Mungo's Hospital for Magical Maladies and Injuries where Neville and his grandmother visit them. (*GOF-30; OOP-23*)

Muggle Law: By federal statute, veterans of active military service are entitled to certain health benefits. The United States Department of Veterans Affairs, which oversees the benefits, operates the nation's largest health care system with 1,400 hospitals, clinics and counseling centers throughout the country. Health care for veterans is not limited to service-connected injuries. Included among the services offered is long-term nursing home care. Co-payments (partial payment for services) by the veteran may be required. The amount varies depending on the veteran's financial situation.

Application to HP Facts: The facts suggest that the Ministry of Magic was paying for the hospital care provided to Mr. and Mrs. Longbottom, presumably in appreciation for their service to the Ministry. This health benefit is similar to that provided to veterans by the United States Government in appreciation of their invaluable service to our country.

* * * * * * * * * * * * * *

Other Areas of Law Implicated by These Facts
Assault and Battery – The Crime
Assault and Battery – The Torts
False Imprisonment
Kidnapping

CHAPTER 88

PERFORMANCE-ENHANCING DRUGS

Don't Worry; Be Happy

HP Facts: At Professor Slughorn's first Potions class, he showed the students a bottle of Felix Felicis. He explained that anyone who drinks the potion will be lucky in everything he attempts for 12 hours. He further explained that Felix Felicis is a banned substance in organized competitions such as sporting events, as well as for examinations and elections. (*HBP–9*)

Muggle Law: Athletes face tremendous pressure to succeed. Winning gains them not only fame and respect, but also fortune. A high salary, prize money, and advertising endorsements can result in a huge income and are typically available only to athletes who excel at their sport. Certain drugs, including the most popular – anabolic steroids, hold out the promise of boosting performance. However, the use of performance enhancing drugs is prohibited by most sports organizations. The primary reasons are that the drugs give users an unfair advantage, plus the drugs threaten athletes' health, and damage a sport's reputation. Winners of sporting events should be determined by athletic talent and accomplishment, not by who has the best drugs.

Banned substances also can cause numerous dangerous side effects. For example, they can mask pain that would otherwise cause an athlete to be sidelined. Unrestricted by the pain, the athlete continues to play while physically compromised and so risks further injury. Additionally, steroids can cause liver cancer, kidney tumors, severe acne, extreme mood swings, trembling, high blood pressure, bad cholesterol, and blood clots that can lead to death. Anabolic steroids have been shown to induce severe mood swings and depression. Professional athletes are customarily required to submit to urine tests which can detect illegal drugs in their system. However, athletes and their trainers have become experts at hiding the use of illegal drugs, either by careful timing or the use of "masking" drugs that render the illegal drugs undetectable. When illegal drugs are detected, penalties include forfeiture of prizes and titles plus suspension from playing in future events. For subsequent incidents, the duration of the suspension increases.

Application to HP Facts: Just as Felix Felicis is banned for sporting events in the Wizarding world, it would likely be prohibited in the Muggle world as well. Its ability to enhance an athlete's achievements provides an unfair advantage to the user.

CHAPTER 89

MARRIAGE

Love, Love Me Do

HP Facts: During the summer after Professor Dumbledore's death, Nymphadora Tonks and Remus Lupin were married. *(DH-4)* Later in the summer, Bill Weasley and Fleur Delacour exchanged wedding vows. The ceremony was held at the Burrow and was conducted by the same wizard who presided over Professor Dumbledore's funeral. *(DH–8)*

Muggle Law: Marriage is the legal union of two people for life. For a valid marriage, certain requirements must be met. They are determined by each state and vary somewhat. However, virtually all states require the following:

- The couple must obtain prior to the ceremony a marriage license issued by a town or court clerk.
- Both parties must be at least 18 years old, or, if younger, have the consent of a parent or a judge.
- Both must be single, widowed, or divorced (no state allows a person to have more than one spouse).
- Each must have sufficient mental capacity to understand the concept of marriage and the accompanying obligations.
- The parties must not be close blood relatives.
- A ceremony must be officiated by a clergy or a judge, and both must say they agree to take each other as husband or wife.
- One or more witnesses must observe the vows.
- Following the ceremony, the marriage license must be recorded in a government office.

Most states require that the parties getting married include one man and one woman. The states that permit same-sex couples to marry are Massachusetts, Connecticut, Iowa, Vermont, New Hampshire, and the District of Columbia. Others may soon be added to the list. Three states permit civil unions, a status that secures some, but not all, of the benefits of marriage. Those states are Hawaii, Illinois and New Jersey.

Additionally, many states require the following: a blood test to determine if the parties have any sexually transmitted diseases (so they can take appropriate steps to avoid spreading the disease to each other or their children); and a waiting period between obtaining the license and the ceremony. This requirement helps to prevent parties from marrying without sufficient thought and preparation or while intoxicated.

Divorce. Unfortunately, not all marriages are made in heaven. Sometimes the parties decide to end their marriage and go their separate ways. The procedure for doing so is called *divorce.* During a divorce, the parties resolve such important issues as custody of children and financial matters, including who pays the bills and how to divide their money and property. Grounds for divorce vary from state to state and typically include some of the following: abandonment for at least one year, adultery, cruel and inhuman treatment, irreconcilable differences, incurable insanity, living apart for a specified period of time (*e.g.,* one year, three years), lengthy imprisonment, and habitual intoxication.

Annulment. An annulment is another procedure that ends a marriage. Whereas a divorce recognizes that a marriage occurred and has been ended, an annulment terminates the marriage as though it never existed. Grounds for annulment vary from state to state and typically include some or all of the following: either party was too young to marry, either party was under the influence of drugs or alcohol at the time of the wedding, either party was mentally incompetent, the parties are close relatives of each other, either party was already married, or one party concealed a drug addiction, prior criminal record, or sexually transmitted disease.

Application to HP Facts: It appears that both couples satisfied the requirements for a valid marriage – sanity, single, not related, proper officiant. Alas, Tonks and Lupin's marriage was cut short by their deaths in the Battle of Hogwarts. We wish Bill and Fleur a long and happy life together.

CHAPTER 90

GOVERNMENT

The Octopus that Is Government

HP Facts: The Ministry of Magic is the governing body of Wizarding society. It is headed by a Minister of Magic. The Ministry is composed of many different administrative agencies. Each has responsibility for a particular aspect of the Wizarding society. For example, there is the Department of Magical Law Enforcement, the Department for the Regulation and Control of Magical Creatures, Improper Use of Magic Office, and the one headed by Ron's dad, the Misuse of Muggle Artifacts Department. Each has regulations that require wizards and witches to refrain from certain conduct.

Violations of these regulations are prosecuted by the relevant department or office. For example, it was the Committee for the Disposal of Dangerous Creatures that notified Hagrid that it would be deciding Buckbeak's fate, and ultimately had the authority to execute the hippogriff. (*POA-11,15*) Likewise, when Dobby used the Hover Charm at the Dursleys' house, it was the Improper Use of Magic Office that issued a violation notice. (*COS-2*)

Legal matters are resolved by a panel of judges called the *Wizengamot. (OOP-8)*

Muggle Law: Like the Wizarding world, countries too have governing bodies. So too do states, counties, cities and towns. Governments in the United States include an elected chief executive, such as the President of the country, the governor of a state, or the mayor of a city. Governments also have elected lawmakers called *legislators*. Their job is to consider and adopt laws. They meet as a body called a *legislature*. An example is our federal legislature - Congress. An additional

227

component of our government is judges. Their role is to enforce the law and resolve disputes.

Our society is quite complex, making it difficult for any one legislature to create laws on all matters within its authority. Therefore, legislators delegate some of their law-making authority to *government agencies*. These are governmental subdivisions responsible for oversight of a specific industry or matter of concern to society. Examples of government agencies include the Occupational Safety and Health Administration, which is concerned with safety of employees at their worksites; the Equal Employment Opportunity Commission, which addresses discrimination in employment; and the Consumer Product Safety Commission, which monitors the safety of goods for sale in stores, such as toys.

Application to HP Facts: The structure of government in the Wizarding world has many parallels to the Muggle world. Both consist of various branches, divisions, and committees to help manage the many issues governments oversee.

Victorious Voldemort

HP Facts: At the very beginning of *Deathly Hallows*, Voldemort and various Death Eaters were sitting at a long table discussing plans for Voldemort's takeover of the Ministry of Magic. Yaxley, one of the Death Eaters and a high ranking Ministry employee, reported that he successfully put the Imperius Curse on Pius Thickness, the Head of the Department of Magical Law Enforcement. Thickness was thus under Voldemort's control. Yaxley advised Voldemort that, with Thickness under their control and Death Eaters in charge at the Department of Magical Transportation, it would be easier to overtake others at the Ministry and overthrow the Minister of Magic, Rufus Scrimgeour. Voldemort insisted that before any attempt was made on Scrimgeour's life, the minister must first be surrounded by Voldemort's supporters. (*DH-1*) Soon thereafter, Harry learned that the Ministry had fallen to Voldemort, Scrimgeour had been killed, and Thickness was the new Minister of Magic. (*DH-8,11*)

Muggle Law: Leaders in the United States are chosen by elections. To win, a majority of voters must select them. Elected officials serve for a specified period of time. When their terms are up, they are either re-elected, in which case they continue in office, or someone else is elected, in which case the former official vacates the office. The change occurs automatically by law without force or violence. For example, the President serves for a four-year term and can be re-elected to a second four-year term (but not a third). When the first term is up, if the President runs for re-election and loses, the President leaves office without incident, and the newly elected chief takes office. If a leader wannabe sought to take office by force, the military would intercede to defeat the interloper and secure the elected official's position.

Application to HP Facts: In the United States, Voldemort would not have been able to gain control of the government by force. Rather, elections would be held to determine who would lead. To gain control, Voldemort and his followers would have been required to run for office and win elections. If Voldemort attempted to take office by force, the police and military would step in and prevent him from doing so.

* * * * * * * * * * * * * *

Other Areas of Law Implicated by These Facts
Conspiracy
Due Process for Animals
Murder

CHAPTER 91

LEGAL TENDER

Cash for the Merchandise

HP Facts: After Harry learned of his acceptance into Hogwarts, Hagrid took him to Diagon Alley to buy school supplies, including robes, a wand, a cauldron, and books. Harry learned that the money used in the Wizarding world is different from the Muggle world and includes Galleons, Sickles and Knuts. The Galleon is the most valuable; Knut the least. It takes 29 Knuts to make a Sickle and 17 Sickles to make a Galleon. (*SS-5)*

Muggle Law: Different countries use different types of money. In every country, money is the *medium of exchange.* This means if you want something – perhaps a new pair of jeans or a computer – you would use money to purchase it.

Sellers of merchandise can restrict the type of money they will accept. So, for example, a seller in the United States can require that payment for goods be made in United States currency. The seller can reject payment attempted in another country's money. The term for this concept is *legal tender.* In the United States, legal tender is dollars and cents. In England, it's pounds, shillings, and pences.

Application to HP Facts: To purchase his wizard paraphernalia and school materials, Harry would need to pay with legal tender of the place where the purchase is made.

CHAPTER 92

ANIMAL USE FOR MEDICAL RESEARCH

What Price for A Second Chance?

HP Facts: As a penalty for fighting, Harry and Draco had to serve a detention with Hagrid. He took them into the Forbidden Forest after dark. Harry and Draco stumbled upon a hooded figure (who we later learn is Voldemort) drinking the blood of a slain unicorn. The figure then advanced swiftly towards Harry, who was frozen in fear. Fortunately, the centaur Firenze appeared and saved Harry by carrying him away. Firenze then explained to Harry that killing a unicorn is a terrible crime. The motivation for doing so is strong – it will keep a wizard alive even if death is imminent but at a horrible price. The duration of the wizard's life is cut in half, and he is forever cursed. (*SS-15*)

Muggle Law: The facts tell us that, in the Wizarding world, a human life can be prolonged by drinking the blood of a unicorn. In the Muggle world, human lives have been saved by the use of laboratory animals in medical research. Certain types of animals can effectively substitute for humans when scientists test medicines and procedures that may hold promise to cure diseases or lessen their effects. Animals used for this purpose include cats, mice, frogs, pigs and monkeys. Researchers must follow laws that minimize injury to the animals. These rules include using only the fewest number of the most appropriate species, treating them humanely, and subjecting them to the least stress possible. Relevant laws mandate details about the day-to-day care of these animals including the size of their cages, temperature of the rooms in which they are kept, best foods, noise level, lighting, and even availability of toys.

Application to HP Facts: In the Muggle world, before a human can kill an animal for its life-saving attributes, other methods to cure the human's ailment must first be attempted in an effort to save the animal. Additionally, when an animal is used to help preserve the life of a human, all relevant laws for the creature's care and comfort must be honored.

* * * * * * * * * * * * *

Other Areas of Law Implicated by These Facts
Cruelty to Animals
Justification

CHAPTER 93

DANGEROUS AND EXOTIC ANIMALS

From Egg to Romania

HP Facts: Hagrid won a dragon egg in a game of cards in Hogsmead Village. He lovingly nurtured it until it hatched. Thus was born Norbert the dragon. Unfortunately for Hagrid, who was very fond of Norbert, the "Warlocks' Convention of 1709" outlawed dragon breeding to prevent Muggles from becoming aware of the Wizarding world. Hagrid was thus forced to send Norbert to Romania where dragons could be kept legally. (*SS-14*)

Additional HP Facts: Harry, Ron, Hermione, and Neville were running from Filch and came across a locked door. Using Harry's wand, Hermione yelled, "alohomora" and the door swung open. They entered and discovered a monstrous dog with three heads, each with drooling saliva hanging from sharp-looking fangs. Harry and his mates turned and ran. We later learn the dog's name was Fluffy, telling us something about the owner's sense of humor. (*SS-9*)

Muggle Law: Many states have laws that prevent people from owning or keeping dangerous animals. The purpose of these laws is to protect people's safety. While the laws vary from state to state, among the circumstances that render an animal dangerous are that it has been trained for animal fighting, it has been trained to be aggressive towards people, or it has a known inclination to be vicious.

Among the animals that cannot be owned or kept are lions, tigers, leopards, cheetahs, hyenas, wolves, coyotes, poisonous or life-threatening reptiles, rats, bats and wild bulls. Certain facilities are, however, allowed to keep such creatures. They

233

include zoos, the circus, research labs, veterinary hospitals and animal refuges.

Application to HP Facts: Hagrid violated the law by maintaining a dragon at Hogwarts. To avoid the various penalties – which in the Muggle world could include jail, fines, liability for medical expenses, and seizure of the animal by the authorities – Hagrid was smart to remove Norbert permanently from Hagrid's home.

The three-headed dog that guarded the room housing the Sorcerer's Stone would be considered a dangerous animal in any state and so keeping him would not be permitted.

* * * * * * * * * * * * *

Other Areas of Law Implicated by These Facts
Gambling
In Loco Parentis
Negligence

CHAPTER 94

DUE PROCESS FOR ANIMALS

A Hippogriff's Appeal

HP Facts: Buckbeak, a hippogriff, "attacked" Draco Malfoy. His father Lucias filed a complaint with the Committee for the Disposal of Dangerous Creatures. Following a hearing, the Committee determined that Buckbeak should be executed. An appeal followed. The appeals judge arrived at the hearing with the executioner, not a good sign. Hagrid and Buckbeak lost the appeal. (*POA-16*)

Muggle Law: The closest legal equivalent in the Muggle world to Buckbeak's experiences with the Committee would be laws applicable to dangerous dogs. Unlike dangerous animals, dogs are generally tame and suitable as pets. Nonetheless, occasionally a canine has a mean disposition with a tendency to bite humans or other animals. Most states permit the euthanizing of such dogs but only after the owner has been extended certain due process rights.

A written complaint must be issued by an animal control officer or a person hurt by the dog. The document is filed with a court or administrative agency charged with implementing dangerous dog laws. A hearing must be promptly scheduled to determine if the dog is, in fact, dangerous. The owner must be informed of the date and time of the hearing, offered the opportunity to present witnesses, and be assigned an impartial judge.

The judge hears the evidence and then decides whether or not the accused canine is, in fact, dangerous. If it is found to be so, the judge can order the animal euthanized. In the alternative, the judge can impose restrictions, such as requiring the owner to always keep the dog indoors or in a securely fenced yard, or requiring that it be muzzled whenever it is outside, and always on a strong leash under the control of a responsible adult. If the dog is thereafter found away from the owner's home, an officer can kill it. If while unrestrained the dog bites someone, the owner may be liable for *treble damages*, meaning three times the actual loss incurred by the injured person. In some states, the judge can order that the animal be sterilized, preventing it from producing puppies. Violations of the judge's directives can result in a fine or jail for the owner.

In most states, the owner has a right to appeal an adverse decision. The appeals court will decide whether the original ruling is supported by sufficient evidence. At the appeal, as with the initial hearing, the dog owner is entitled to an objective judge.

Application to HP Facts: Buckbeak and Hagrid initially received the due process to which they were entitled. Hagrid was given notice of the hearing, time to prepare his case, and an opportunity at that proceeding to present evidence in favor of "Beekey." While Hagrid was also granted an appeal, the impartiality of the appeals judge is suspect given that he brought the executioner with him to the proceeding. A biased judge would violate Hagrid and Buckbeak's due process rights.

* * * * * * * * * * * * *

Other Areas of Law Implicated by These Facts
Appeals
Dangerous and Exotic Animals
Government
Right to an Unbiased Judge

CHAPTER 95

DANGEROUS AND EXOTIC PLANTS

Perilous Plants

HP Facts: Harry, Ron, and Hermione reported for the first Herbology class of their second year at Hogwarts. It was held in greenhouse three. This location contained "far more interesting and dangerous plants" than greenhouse one. Professor Sprout informed the class that they would be repotting Mandrakes and asked if anyone could explain their characteristics. Of course, Hermione was prepared to answer and explained that Mandrakes were used to restore "people who had been transfigured or cursed to their original state." Unfortunately, the cry of the Mandrake is fatal to anyone who hears it. Fortunately, the Mandrakes the class would be working with were very young and by wearing earmuffs, students could avoid death. (*COS-6*)

Additional HP Facts: While visiting Mr. Weasley at St. Mungo's Hospital for Magical Maladies and Injuries, Harry observed one of the Healers delivering a potted plant to a patient named Broderick Bode, a Ministry of Magic employee. The Healer set the plant down on the bedside cabinet next to Broderick. The plant was rather ugly with long swaying tentacles. (*OOP-23*) Several days later, Harry, Ron, and Hermione read an article in the *Daily Prophet* that reported that Bode was found dead having been strangled by the potted plant. It turns out that the plant was Devil's Snare, a deadly plant that tightens its grip on its victims by squeezing and eventually strangling them. (*OOP-25*)

Muggle Law: A variety of plants present various dangers and so are outlawed. The risks they present include:

- Some are poisonous and can kill.
- The sap from some can cause burns, scarring and chronic dermatitis, a rash-like condition of the skin.
- Some are diseased and can spread the illness.
- Some attract damaging or dangerous insects.
- The possession of some is criminal, such as marijuana.
- Various aquatic plants expand and grow rapidly threatening fish and other underwater wildlife, clog waterways, impede navigation, and cause disease.

To protect people, animals, and other plants from these threats, the Federal Government and some states have adopted laws to prohibit or restrict certain plants from being grown in the United States, imported from other countries, transported by common carriers (buses, planes, trains, and trucks), sent through the mail, bought or sold, or possessed. If these laws are violated, police can seize the offending plant and destroy it. The wrongdoer may face criminal liability if he knew the plant possessed dangerous qualities.

Application to HP Facts: Given the hazards associated with Mandrakes and Devil's Snare, these would likely be among the plants illegal to possess. If so, Sprout could be prosecuted criminally for having the Mandrakes and insisting students interact with them. Concerning the Healer, it appears she did not know the plant delivered to Bode was Devils Snare. Since she did not knowingly possess the dangerous plants, she would not be criminally liable.

* * * * * * * * * * * * * *

Other Areas of Law Implicated by These Facts
In Loco Parentis
Murder
Negligence

CHAPTER 96

LOBBYING

Can't Buy Me Love, No

HP Facts: Immediately after Harry's school suspension hearing at the Ministry of Magic, Harry and Mr. Weasley saw Lucias Malfoy in the hallway waiting for the Minister of Magic. Harry asked Mr. Weasley why Lucias was there. Mr. Weasley responded that Lucias had given gold to all sorts of Ministry-related events and causes for years, getting in return access to the "right people." Per Mr. Weasley, giving this gold enabled Lucias to ask for favors including delaying the passage of laws he did not like. (*OOP-9*)

Muggle Law: In politics, there is an expression called "Pay to Play." It refers to a scorned practice of elected officials granting favors, such as lucrative contracts, to individuals, businesses and organizations, in exchange for large political contributions. The practice is frowned upon for the unfair benefit it gives to donors and the corrupting effect it can have on politics. Yet the cost to run a campaign is big and continues to grow. The more money required, the greater the potential influence large donors have on candidates, elected officials, and public policy.

Numerous laws seek to restrict the influence money has in campaigns. Agencies exist to regulate and control campaign contributions. Many nongovernmental "watchdog groups" have been formed to monitor campaign donations and publicize those that appear inappropriate.

A legitimate method of influencing legislators to pass a bill or, in the alternative, not to adopt it, is called *lobbying*. This refers to attempts to convince members of a legislature of the merits or failings of proposed laws. For example, the state in which

240

you live may be debating whether to adopt a law that would prohibit drivers from using cell phones in a car except when using a hands-free device. Assume you work for a company that manufactures hands-free devices. You would likely want to join forces with other manufacturers to lobby for passage of the proposed law.

An example of an organization that might benefit from lobbying to advance its positions is S.P.E.W. (Society for the Protection of Elfish Welfare). Hermione could lobby the Ministry to pass a law that would mandate payment of wages to house elves.

The term *lobbyist* refers to a person who lobbies for a cause on behalf of a group or organization. Lobbyists do much more than attempt to persuade legislators. They research and analyze proposed legislation, attend legislative hearings, monitor developments of a bill, keep their clients apprised, work with coalitions who share the same views, and educate legislators and others about the implications of proposed legislation.

Various laws restrict the actions of lobbyists including significant limitations on the amount of gifts or money they can give to public officials.

Application to HP Facts: If Lucias lived in a state that restricted campaign contributions, his influence would be appropriately lessened. Lucias would still be able to lobby legislators to seek support for his position on proposed laws. However, appropriately, he would have to convince lawmakers based more on the merits of his position and less on the amount of money he contributed.

* * * * * * * * * * * * *

Other Areas of Law Implicated by These Facts
Freedom of Speech

CHAPTER 97

GOVERNMENT-MANDATED REGISTRATION

Sign Up Here

HP Facts: The Ministry of Magic requires Animagi (wizards who are able to transform into animals; the singular is Animagus) to register with the Ministry. This means the Animagi must provide certain information that is kept on record. The data required include the particular animal into which the registrant transforms and a description of the animal's markings. The information enables the Ministry to keep tabs on the Animagi. Having Animagus capabilities is rare. Some of the characters in the Wizarding world who we know are Animagi include Sirius Black (dog), Peter Pettigrew (rat), James Potter (stag), and Rita Skeeter (beetle). All of them ignored the law and failed to register. Professor McGonagall (cat) did, however, register. (*POA-18*)

Muggle Law: Federal and state laws require that certain categories of people register with the government. Among those required to do so are males of an age eligible to be drafted by the military (true, although we do not currently have a draft), lobbyists (people who attempt to sway government officials' votes), and aliens (people who are citizens of other countries but living in the United States).

Another category is sex offenders. These are people who have been convicted of child sexual molestation and sexually violent offenses. They must report their names, addresses, and other identifying information to their local law enforcement agency. If they move, they must re-register with their new local police department. The requirement is based on studies that show sex offenders have a high rate of committing additional sex crimes. The resulting registry is an important source of information to the public and law enforcement about the whereabouts and proximity of convicted sex offenders. It enables parents, schools, and day care centers to better protect children.

The law mandating registration of sex offenders is called the Wetterling Act and was passed by Congress in 1994. A related federal statute called Megan's Law was enacted two years later and requires states to make available to the public the information on the registry. Both laws were named for youngsters who tragically were abducted and sexually abused.

If a sexual predator fails to register, he thereby commits a federal felony that can result in years in jail. Some states have laws that go one step further. They require not just that the information be available to people who ask, but rather that the police take the affirmative step of notifying people and institutions in the vicinity of a sex offender's home. Examples of methods used to make the notification include door-to-door canvass, direct mail, fax, and email.

Application to HP Facts: Like the Muggle sex offender law and related registration laws, the Animagus registration requirement allows the Ministry to keep a closer eye on a limited population that potentially threatens the safety of wizards and witches. This objective is achieved only if those required to register, in fact, do so. The failure by Black, Skeeter, Pettigrew and Harry's father could have resulted in their prosecution for a serious crime and substantial jail time.

CHAPTER 98

EMERGENCY RESTRICTIONS

Lock Down

HP Facts: Following the attacks on Muggle-borns by the Heir of Slytherin, Hogwarts adopted new restrictions on students' activities to protect their safety. Included among the restrictions was a 6:00 p.m. curfew. Students were also forbidden from going to and from classes without a teacher escort, and they could not use the bathrooms without a teacher present. All Quidditch practices and matches were postponed (much to Oliver Wood's great disappointment). (*COS-14*)

Additional HP Facts: Sirius Black was on the loose. Signs from the Ministry were posted around Hogsmead advising residents and visitors that dementors would be patrolling after dark. Shoppers were advised to complete their purchases before nightfall.
(*POA-10*)

Additional HP Facts: At the very beginning of *Order of the Phoenix*, the town of Little Whinging was in the midst of a drought. Therefore, the use of hoses was prohibited and residents of Privet Drive were unable to wash their cars or water their lawns. (*OOP-1*)

Muggle Law: The ultimate duty of governments is to protect the public's safety and health. To do so, governments have certain authority when faced with emergencies. Included in this authority is the right to temporarily impose necessary restrictions on fundamental liberties, including freedom of movement.

Among the emergencies that trigger this authority are terrorist attacks, natural disasters such as a flood, hurricane or tsunami, outbreaks of contagious diseases, riots and violent protests, uncontrolled fires and shortages of essential resources. Restrictions on the public's activities may be necessary to enable any of the following government responses to a crisis: sending needed rescuers, equipment or supplies; preventing the spread of a contagious disease; identifying and halting would-be terrorists; restoring law and order when riots erupt; or preserving essential resources. Similar to a government's responsibility for the public's safety, a school is responsible for the safety of its students. This responsibility is based on a rule of law called *in loco parentis* which means "in place of a parent." The school, too, can impose restrictions in the face of an emergency as necessary to safeguard pupils.

Application to HP Facts: When an emergency occurs, a government or school can take drastic measures to protect the safety of those who attend. The measures adopted, however, must be reasonably necessary to manage the threat. Since several Hogwarts students had already been attacked, the school had good reason to believe others were at risk. Hogwarts, thus, was justified in imposing safety measures such as requiring that students be escorted by faculty whenever they were outside their dorms or a classroom and requiring students to remain in their dormitories in the evenings. Similarly, when the Ministry believed an escaped killer was on the loose, the Ministry was justified in instituting restrictions in Hogsmead to safeguard residents and visitors.

Concerning the drought, water is a necessary resource for drinking, bathing, cooking and household chores. When its availability is threatened, governments can prohibit non-essential uses. Whinging's restrictions were reasonable under the circumstances.

* * * * * * * * * * * * *

Other Areas of Law Implicated by These Facts

In Loco Parentis

245

CHAPTER 99

IMPORT/EXPORT LAWS

The Right Size Fits All

HP Facts: After graduation from Hogwarts, Percy Weasley went to work for the Ministry of Magic in the Department of International Magical Cooperation. One of his first tasks was to write a report regarding the standardization of cauldron thickness. The Ministry had become aware that some of the foreign imports were too thin, resulting in leaks. Percy was concerned that unless some kind of uniform international standards were imposed, the market would be flooded with substandard products. (*GOF-5*)

Muggle Law: Imported products must meet certain standards set by national and international laws. The goals of these laws are many and include protecting health and safety of humans and animals, protecting the environment, preventing the introduction into the country of foreign parasites and animal diseases, preserving endangered species, and more.

Examples of mandated standards for imports include:

- Limitations on the use of chemicals, additives, contaminants, and toxins from beverages and growing crops
- Compliance with required techniques of production and avoidance of prohibited methods (for example no slave labor, lead paint or poisonous materials)
- Compliance with food labeling rules that may require such information as place of origin, production method, and nutritional or medical information
- Standards for organic fruits and vegetables

- Compliance with sanitation regulations

Application to HP Facts: Percy was on the right track. If imported cauldrons were defective, a law to mandate standards to eliminate the problem is in order. Percy could, for example, encourage the Ministry to adopt minimum standards of thickness that all imported cauldrons must meet. If cauldrons were thereafter delivered that failed to satisfy the required thickness, the Ministry or the business importing the products could reject them and ship them back to the seller.

What's a Genie to Do?

HP Facts: In his capacity working for the Ministry's Misuse of Muggle Artifacts Department, Mr. Weasley enforced a restriction on the importation into Britain of flying carpets. This dismayed Ali Bashir, a merchant from another country, who wanted to export them to England, believing a market existed for their use as family vehicles. (*GOF-7*)

Muggle Law: The United States and most other countries bar various products from being imported. The reasons for the prohibitions are numerous and include the same reasons for imposing standards on imported products. Examples of products that are prohibited from entering the United States include: dangerous toys, vehicles that do not protect passengers in a crash, and illegal substances such as narcotic drugs. Some products are *restricted* but not *prohibited*. These require a special license or permit from a federal agency before they can be imported. Examples include certain fruits, vegetables, and pets, as well as guns.

Application to HP Facts: Manufactures may envision a foreign market for merchandise and want to export products to tap that market. However, if the items are on the list of goods that cannot be imported into the country of destination, the products' entry would be illegal. In the Wizarding world, flying carpets were on the list. Mr. Weasley was duty-bound to enforce the prohibition. Bashir will have to devise another scheme for making money.

* * * * * * * * * * * * *

Other Areas of Law Implicated by These Facts
Government

APPENDICES

Appendix A

INTRODUCTION TO LAW

DEFINITION. What is this thing called law? Perhaps the most understandable definition is this: a body of rules that people must comply with or face penalties. Additional meanings include a set of rules used by judges to decide disputes and a method to control people's conduct. Common to all of these definitions is the idea that law affects our life everyday in a significant way. Law requires that we conform our conduct to certain expected rules and if we do not, we face unpleasant consequences.

SOURCES OF LAW. From where does our law come? There are four sources:

- The Federal Constitution
- Statutes adopted by legislators
- Common law created by judges
- Government agency regulations

CONSTITUTIONAL LAW. The law embodied in the United States Constitution is called Constitutional Law. It prescribes the organization of the federal government – including the executive, legislative and judicial branches – and defines the powers of the federal government. The Constitution establishes vital legal rights, called the Bill of Rights. These include freedom of speech, freedom of religion, right to a fair trial, right to an attorney, right against cruel and unusual treatment, and more.

STATUTES. These are laws promulgated by *legislators* who are elected law makers. We vote for legislators at the federal, state, and local levels. Each level of government has different topics on which they *legislate* (make laws). For example, the Federal Government legislates on such issues as national security, federal crimes (criminal activity involving more than one state, such as kidnapping a person and transporting him across state lines), and business transactions that impact more

250

than one state. State legislators pass laws addressing matters such as speed limits on state roads, state crimes (criminal activity occurring only in one state) and child neglect and abuse. Local legislators adopt laws dealing with such topics as requiring dogs to be on a leash when away from their owners' property and restrictions on the permissible noise level at a home or business.

COMMON LAW. This refers to legal rules that originate in judges' decisions.

GOVERNMENT AGENCY REGULATIONS. *Government agencies* are governmental subdivisions. They are created because our society is very complex and legislators cannot be expected to have the required expertise to adopt laws on all facets of life. Each agency oversees a particular industry and may have law-making authority for that specific industry. Examples include the Consumer Product Safety Commissions, which enforces regulations designed to ensure the safety of consumer products, and the Environmental Protection Agency, which is charged with safeguarding our environment. The term *regulations* refers to law created by a government agency.

Appendix B

DIFFERENCES BETWEEN CIVIL AND CRIMINAL LAW

All law can be classified as either *criminal* or *civil*. The four main differences between the two, explained in detail below, are 1) the remedy sought, 2) the name of the plaintiff, 3) the attorney for the plaintiff, and 4) the burden of proof.

REMEDY.   In a criminal case, the remedy sought by the plaintiff is punishment of the wrongdoer. In a civil case, the remedy is compensation (payment) for an injury.

NAME OF PLAINTIFF.   There are often two parties to a lawsuit, although there may be more. They are generally called the *plaintiff* and the *defendant*. The plaintiff is the one who has a complaint against the defendant and initiates the lawsuit. The defendant is the party who the plaintiff sues, seeking a remedy. In a criminal case, the plaintiff is society-at-large, not just the victim.   The plaintiff's name in every criminal case is "The People of the State of _____" or "The Commonwealth of _____."   In a civil case, the name of the plaintiff is the person who was harmed.

PLAINTIFF'S ATTORNEY.   In a criminal case, society is represented by a prosecutor, often called a district attorney. Prosecutors' salaries are paid by the government.   In a civil case, the person suing hires and pays for his own lawyer.

BURDEN OF PROOF. In both civil and criminal cases, the plaintiff, to win, must convince the jury of the truth of his claims to a specified degree of certainty. In a criminal case, the degree required is *beyond a reasonable doubt*. This is a very high standard. If a juror has any reasonable doubt (more than a whim or guess), the juror must vote for not guilty. In a civil case, the burden of proof is significantly less.   It is a *preponderance of the evidence* and means that the jury's degree of certainty that plaintiff should win the case need only be more than 50 percent. The reason for the difference is that in a criminal case, a person's *freedom* is at stake, while in a civil case, only *money* is at risk. As a society, we value freedom much more than money.

Appendix C

CRIMINAL LAW ISSUES

Understanding some aspects of criminal law will facilitate your understanding of this book. Discussed in this Appendix are the following: 1) the difference between felonies and misdemeanors; 2) sentencing; 3) degreeing factors; and 4) defenses.

FELONY AND MISDEMEANOR. Crimes are divided into two categories for purposes of distinguishing serious conduct from less serious conduct. A *felony* is the more serious crime. The time in jail faced by a perpetrator who commits a felony is more than one year and could be life. Examples of felonies include assault resulting in serious injury, grand larceny (stealing a large amount of money; in some states, more than $1,000.00), and robbery (stealing from a person by the use of force).

A *misdemeanor* is a lower level crime for which the maximum time in jail is one year. Examples of misdemeanors include stealing limited amounts of money, hitting a person causing injury but not serious injury, and the first time someone is convicted of driving while intoxicated (DWI) (in some states, a second conviction is a felony). A third category of wrongful conduct exists in criminal law called a *violation*. It involves illegal behavior less serious than a misdemeanor. Usually the maximum jail time is 15 days. An example is *harassment,* which includes pushing or shoving someone, without causing injury.

SENTENCING. Following conviction in a criminal case, the judge will sentence the defendant. The sentence may consist of several components, including a fine, jail, probation, community service, alcohol or drug treatment, and anger management counseling. A judge has considerable discretion. Among the factors that will influence the sentence are whether the defendant has a criminal record; the consequence of the crime on the victim; and the defendant's circumstances, such as health, employment, family, addictions; and how serious was the crime. For example, a defendant who steals a $900.00 laptop will likely receive a harsher sentence than a defendant who steals $10.00 worth of food at a food court, although both crimes are misdemeanors.

DEGREEING FACTORS. Most crimes have *degreeing factors.* These are circumstances that make the crime more serious. Examples of degreeing factors include the seriousness of an injury, the amount of money stolen, the use of a weapon while committing the crime, and prior conviction(s) for the same crime.

DEFENSES. A *defense* is an explanation for illegal conduct that relieves the actor from liability. An example is self-defense. Customarily, if you use force against another person and cause injury, you may be liable for the crime of assault. However, if the reason you used the force was to defend yourself from an attack, a defense of self-defense may apply, which would result in the charges being dismissed.

Appendix D

COURT JURISDICTION

The term *jurisdiction* refers to the authority of a court to hear cases. Most courts have limited authority, meaning they hear only certain types of lawsuits. For example, family court has jurisdiction to hear cases involving family issues such as adoption or child neglect. It does not have jurisdiction to hear a case about a plaintiff who tripped and fell in a restaurant and is seeking compensation for a broken arm.

There are numerous classifications of jurisdiction that courts can have. Two of them are original and appellate jurisdiction. Original jurisdiction refers to the authority of a court to hear cases when they are brought to court for the first time. Trials are held in courts of original jurisdiction. Appellate jurisdiction refers to the authority of a court to hear appeals. An *appeal* is the process where a court with appellate jurisdiction reviews the decision of the court that previously heard the case. The appellate court can affirm the prior court's decision (uphold it), reverse the decision, or return the case to the original court for further proceedings.

Made in the USA
Middletown, DE
02 December 2021